Words in a Journey of Care

Lynn M. Butterbrodt

ISBN: 1511736739
ISBN 13: 9781511736732

For my miracles,
Devin, Randy, and Mariah

Contents

Preface

EACH OF US has a story. Words are what we have to share, move forward with, season life with, and remember. I am the beneficiary of a story about life and death, an experience that, at times, went beyond words. Because of my integral role in my husband's cancer journey, many words have deeper meaning. *Words in a Journey of Care* draws from my experience. The one- or two-word chapter titles are the red threads that drive the theme of each chapter. The book doesn't follow chronological order but spirals in a forward direction. Events from an ordinary life are intermingled with overwhelming circumstances, capturing the reality that life and its cycles are ongoing, even as a situation can be mentally and physically all consuming.

These chapters tell a story of pain, heartbreak, and restitution set within the worlds of medicine and faith and seasoned with a lot of love. I will always be grateful for the love that surrounded us on this journey. May *Words in a Journey of Care* enhance and embrace your story in ways that give meaning to your words and peace to your life.

Thank you to all who have embraced me as an author: to all who read my online journal; to those who edited my first manuscript, providing valuable input and encouragement; to Maren Tirabassi for guidance in rewriting the manuscript and advice about publishing it. I have been blessed.

Introduction

TWO HUNDRED MILES away from my home in Clarence, Iowa, there is a restaurant called the Canadian Honker. It's across the street from Saint Mary's Hospital in Rochester, Minnesota. Whether for a meal, a coffee break, dessert, or just a different atmosphere, this restaurant is a respite for folks who want to step away from the hospital setting. My husband, Ross, spent a lot of time in three separate hospitals between November 2009 and September 2010. He was an inpatient at Saint Mary's Hospital for sixty-five days and an outpatient for many others.

When Ross was at Saint Mary's, I would go to the Canadian Honker for comfort food by myself, with our kids, or with visitors who came to see Ross. Folks like us who are familiar with the place simply call it "the Honker." It became a favorite place, very dear to me. Homelike. I could feel my spirits lift slightly just by saying the word *honker*.

The Honker is the home of Rochester's famous and award winning cake known as Bunnie's Coconut Cake: a luscious white cake lavished with coconut milk, whipping cream, and shredded coconut. It was served in huge squares. I never met Bunnie, but this cake that holds her name became my ultimate comfort food.

The Honker was the location for the most difficult conversation I've ever had. It took place before our evening meal on July 3, 2010. Devin,

Randy, and Mariah—my children—were my dining guests. Ross was asleep in his hospital room across the street. For all intents and purposes, we appeared normal. Our heavy hearts weren't outwardly visible.

There were parts of our lives that were normal. Devin was a senior in college and enjoying a summer internship with a company in Michigan. He had flown to Rochester to be with us. Devin—the thinker, builder, and creator, a man of few but articulate and important words. Randy had just graduated from high school and was preparing to start college. Randy—compassionate and sensitive, filled with a generous spirit, Ross's mirror image. Mariah was about to start high school. Her smile and personality brightened even the darkest room. Mariah—beautiful inside and out.

My life at the time revolved around the three of them and the man sleeping in the hospital bed across the street. My job was on hold, my home was being managed by my parents, and all else was set aside. I communicated with the outside world through daily entries in an online journal, and I was nourished by online responses.

That evening at the Honker, I sat at the table with my kids, in awe of how they were growing and who they were becoming. We ordered our food. Randy ordered the roast beef special, Devin ordered ribs, and Mariah ordered a cheeseburger and cottage cheese. Pasta for me. I remember the details. The restaurant was crowded, yet it seemed as if we were the only ones there. The conversation we were about to have was necessary. The topic was cancer. I knew it would be best to talk before dark, while the sun was still shining in the evening sky. This wasn't a bedtime conversation.

While waiting for our food, I tried to start the conversation. I asked if they had any questions about what was going on with Dad. No. I asked again with new words. No. We sat. Randy broke the silence by asking a question about chemotherapy. I blurted out an answer and then reminded them their dad's cancer would not be cured, but its progression could possibly be slowed. That was the best we could hope for. The boys understood.

Mariah said, "So, that means Dad will have cancer for the rest of his life."

I said, "Yes."

Randy said, "Mariah." And that's all he could say.

I swallowed the lump in my throat and explained, "Yes, Dad will have cancer for the rest of his life, and unfortunately the rest of his life probably won't be long."

Tears welled up in her eyes, and Mariah began to cry. She sobbed, and I held her. The boys sat silently, sadly. I questioned myself and what my words had done at this time and in this place.

Our food came, and the server awkwardly set plates in front of each of us. It struck me that this scene was probably familiar at the Honker.

Mariah was begging to leave, but I said, "No." She sat on my lap, and the four of us stared at one another. Four of us—not five of us.

This had been our sanctuary, safe and holy ground, and now it was a place my children wanted to leave. The food was cooling. Time stood still. The immediacy consumed us as we sat at that table, and all that surrounded us seemed invisible.

Then Devin began to eat. Randy began to pick at his food. Mariah announced that she didn't want to eat, and Randy announced he was forcing himself. I held Mariah. We sat. We stared. We sighed sighs too deep for human understanding.

Perhaps it was then that the Holy Spirit interceded. Devin picked up a rib and smeared barbeque sauce across his face. Sweet distraction! Mariah burst into laughter. She pulled away from my embrace and sat up. I began to eat. I suggested she eat some cottage cheese, and she did. Then she ate the cheeseburger.

On that evening, at the table in that sanctuary, we broke down and built up. Refreshed, we returned to Ross's hospital room. I realized that that conversation was a prelude to many difficult discussions. Important work happened at that table.

On that particular day, it was nearly impossible to remember a time when conversations were carefree and untroubled, when our words didn't carry the heaviness associated with serious illness, when life was lighter and the journey easier.

We were high school sweethearts, Ross and I. He was a few years older than I was. We married while I was in college. Four years later, we started our family. Devin, our oldest, was followed by Randy and then Mariah, at four-year intervals. Order.

Ross's agricultural career was not just a job; it was a passion. He had many passions. He loved everything he did—from running the pump for the fire department to tinkering in the garage, from coaching baseball to fishing, from mowing the lawn to making up silly songs, from finding deals on eBay to celebrating anything with friends and family. He loved the people who were in his life and always made time to visit. Because he was a champion visitor, he usually ran late—for everything. His lateness only bothered me.

Looking back, I wonder if we appreciated the ordinary in our days, months, and years when we were living them. Our story was traditional; we lived the vows: in sickness and in health, for better or worse, in plenty and in want, until death parts us.

The story I'm sharing isn't about our ordinary, traditional life. It's about life not going as planned, about adaptations and recovery.

As you prepare to glimpse a life-changing time with me, imagine a box. There is a portion of my life that can't be contained, yet I can imagine it in a metaphorical box. This book is about what's inside. It's about Ross; it's about me; it's about our kids; and it's about an experience that was shared by a multitude of folks: family, friends, health care professionals, and strangers. The box is open. As the contents spill out, dear reader, may you find pieces of this journey to take with you on your own travels. I write especially for those who have been forever changed by a life experience that, perhaps in all of its ugliness, became a thing of indescribable beauty.

Ross's Story

THIS IS NOT unusual. It's 3:23 a.m. on November 1, 2010, and I'm awake. The human brain can be supercharged in the darkness, in that time between one day and the next. Life holds greater mystery in the dark, and meaning can evolve from mystery. My creativity and clarity can peak during the wee hours. I've discovered that these are the hours when reality can be distorted, emotions can be askew, and time can seemingly stand still.

At this particular time, on this particular day, I wake up thinking about "middle-earth" and the way a friend defined this term for me. In her e-mail dated September 10, 2010, at 7:02 a.m., she stated, "That's what I call the world between heaven and our usual reality." She went on to say that my family had been living within her definition of middle-earth for almost a week.

That definition seemed fitting at the time, and as I wake up on this particular morning and middle-earth enters my dancing mind, it seems so right for this time as well. It is definitely where life was for us on that particular September day, and this middle-earth is also where we have lived for quite some time. Middle-earth has held us as our lives became forever changed.

My husband, Ross, died at 9:39 p.m. on September 10, 2010, fourteen hours after I received the middle-earth e-mail.

The waning crescent moon is smiling at me right now. The stars are shining brightly. I am wide-awake, and it is story time.

• • •

November 1, 2009, was All Saints' Day, a day celebrated with tradition at our church. With love and remembrance, those who passed away during the year were named, as candles were lit and a bell tolled during a powerful, grace-filled communion service. At the time, I was the associate pastor. Worship services, such as those on All Saints' Day, remind me of the privilege of the call to ministry, a stressful, arduous labor of love.

Empowered by worship, I went home from church, and that afternoon my husband and I said tearful good-byes to our family and traveled 204 miles north to Rochester, Minnesota, home of the Mayo Clinic. I began my online journal on that day with a simple statement that we had arrived at Mayo, and we were in awe. At the time, I was unaware how the time ahead would unfold and how the yet-unwritten words of my online journal would become a lifeline of sorts.

Ross's body was ill. Ross's story was complicated.

In 1963 Ross was diagnosed with a Wilms tumor (childhood kidney cancer). His left kidney was removed, and subsequent treatment consisted of heavy doses of radiation. My heart aches for all that Ross, his parents, and his family endured. In the 1960s, children died from Wilms tumors. It was rare that a child lived after having this cancer. The only kids who survived were those who received heavy doses of radiation. The surgery and radiation treatments that followed saved his life, but as Ross aged, his radiated tissue changed. The radiation caused deformation in his torso, thinning of tissue, diminishing bone quality, and narrowing of important digestive and circulatory passages. In the 1960s radiation treatment did not pinpoint cancer cells. Ross had a burned rectangle on his abdomen, roughly six inches by four inches, representing the hole in the lead apron he had worn when being treated. The hole had allowed rays to pass through his body from front to back. This radiation field included not only the area of his cancer, but the surrounding tissue. The burned rectangle was also visible on his back.

Ross had received treatments for three years. Ross was among the earliest cancer survivors from the University of Iowa Hospitals and Clinics (UIHC). He lived with gratitude and a sense of accomplishment. An educational component was a by-product of his case. Ross contributed to the world of medicine.

Throughout the time I knew Ross, his survivor gratitude was intertwined with trepidation. There were times during his life that he harbored toxic fear of cancer returning to his body. From the outside, one would not have known this.

In 1989 the term *radiation damage* entered our lives and became a constant in our household vocabulary. In that year, due to radiation damage, he had nearly twelve inches of his large intestine removed. His doctors were amazed that decades had passed without complications. After his surgery, record had been made of a section of small intestine that would likely cause problems in the future.

In 2004 Ross began having complications involving his spine that required back surgery. Epidural fat, a by-product of radiated tissue, was accumulating around his spinal cord with the threat of irreversible damage if not treated. In October 2004 he had a nontraditional lumbar laminectomy to remove the epidural fat. A week after surgery, he was diagnosed with a staph infection, so his incision was reopened and the infection was eradicated. The infection had likely been harbored in radiated tissue. The wound did not heal; it opened. A wound vacuum, a hyperbaric oxygen chamber, and a peripherally inserted central catheter (PICC line) for antibiotics were the integral parts of the treatment plan that was put into place.

Unfortunately, Ross's entire venous system from his chest downward filled with blood clots. Wound healing was put on hold as the life-threatening deep vein thrombosis issue was addressed. Four vascular surgeries followed. Two stents were placed in his inferior vena cava (the large vein that returns blood to the heart from the lower half of the body), which was narrowed and damaged due to radiation. The narrowed area actually saved his life at the time. Acting as a filter, the severe narrowing prevented the clots from moving into his chest. Radiation damage to his aorta was also noted. Ross was given a prescription for Coumadin, a blood thinner, to be taken for the rest of his life.

When the blood-clot issues were resolved and the risk had passed, the process of healing and closing his back wound was resumed. Six months later, after more hyperbaric oxygen, wound-vac therapy, and PICC line antibiotics, a skin flap and graft surgery followed. Until this time, three vertebrae could be seen through the opening on his back. He would lie on our bed while I changed the various dressings on his back. This was not a scene I would have ever imagined when life was normal.

Ross's health and poor healing consumed us in that very trying year. Devin was a junior in high school. Randy was in seventh grade, and Mariah was in third grade. We had an incredible support system.

In 2007 Ross had acute gallstone pancreatitis. Two procedures to remove the gallstones were required on his pancreas, and his gallbladder had to be removed. All went well, but he was left with a compromised pancreas. His condition restricted him from drinking alcohol. Due to deteriorating spinal problems, he also had a ten-pound lifting restriction. With these restrictions, Ross had to relinquish some normalcy as he knew it. Accepting the adjusted lifestyle was difficult. He was forced to yield to serious, chronic, and life-altering conditions. It was not easy for him to obey his doctors' orders, but he knew that disobeying would lead to worse circumstances.

In May 2009 Ross began having severe upper-gastrointestinal discomfort and vomited nearly every day. Those words from the doctor in 1989 rang in our heads: "There's a section of small intestine that will likely cause problems in the future." Between May and October of 2009, many tests were performed to determine the cause of his illness, beginning with the least stressful and invasive for his compromised body. Given Ross's history, testing was risky, and some tests were impossible for reasons such as his vena cava stents and lack of a kidney. Ultrasounds, x-rays, nuclear scans, enterography, and more did not reveal the source of his problem. However, these tests gave doctors many views of Ross's severely injured tissue. Then came an enteroclysis test, where a thin tube was placed through his nose and swallowed. This tube was to pass into the small intestine and have a barium solution forced through it. But the tube would not go into the small intestine. The problem was discovered. Ross had a severe stricture in his duodenum, at the worst possible location imaginable. The stricture provided only a two-millimeter clearance from his duodenum to his jejunum (sections of small intestine). Normally, this area should measure two to three centimeters. We got an answer, but needless to say, that was a very bad day. Ross was miserable before, during, and after the enteroclysis test, and the answer was not good news.

Doctors at UIHC attempted a balloon procedure to stretch the constricted area. A surgeon was available in case the tissue tore during the procedure. Thankfully, the tissue didn't tear, but it also didn't stretch. The word used to describe his tissue was *friable*. There was an obvious problem.

Ross embarked on a difficult trek in 2009, and his journey affected each of us. He was referred to the Mayo Clinic in Rochester from UIHC in Iowa City. On November 9, 2009, he had a complicated surgery, rerouting his small intestine to bypass the constriction. Surgeons explored and repaired for hours. Radiation damage was the culprit.

He spent time in intensive care following this surgery and did well in his recovery but only for a short time. An intestinal leak developed, causing a serious and painful infection.

He had begun hyperbaric treatments for healing. Because of the infection, those treatments came to an abrupt end, as did nourishment by mouth. A Hickman catheter (a central line placed in his chest) replaced the PICC line in his arm. The Hickman was his life-line for total parenteral nutrition (TPN) and antibiotics. Along with the Hickman and an unhealed abdominal incision, he had three tubes placed: one into his stomach, one into his small intestine, and one draining his abdomen of infection (specifically, a g-tube, a j-tube, and a radiology drain). Each had a purpose, and each required care. We dealt with bile in huge, measured quantities. While I was measuring bile output, more of those *I never could have imagined this* thoughts would enter my mind.

There were times when the scope of this experience was almost unfathomable. Effects rippled through many circles of the people to whom we were connected. Our children grew in life-changing ways, showing incredible strength and compassion. In a difficult time, their three unique personalities provided wisdom and clarity, along with some much-needed humor.

Both Ross and I had disappeared from the daily grind as we knew it. We were indebted to our parents for their never-ending love, sup-port, and care. The understanding of our employers and community went beyond measure.

Ross's acceptance of his situation was exceptional, and many members of his health care team remarked about his high level of cooperation, his patience, and his good attitude. He presented them with real challenges and dilemmas, however. Day by day, sometimes hour by hour, we dealt with it all. In a really, really bad time, we were the recipients of goodness.

The calendar turned to 2010. Healing problems, digestive prob-lems, infections, complications, unease, hospitalizations, and finan-cial burdens elevated. *I cannot believe this is my life* was a thought that ran through my mind on a daily basis.

We were feeling depleted in body, mind, and spirit. Then we were blessed with the month of May. We enjoyed a small reprieve from the seriousness of our situation, and we were able to celebrate milestone events in our family. Truly, May 2010 was a gift.

Ross's problems escalated very quickly in June, and we were blind-sided by his cancer diagnosis. More procedures and tubes followed, along with an even more heightened care plan and major decisions. "My cancer is back," Ross said soberly upon hearing the initial diag-nosis. "This is not going to end well" were his words after learning of the invasive, fast-growing cancer he had. The pernicious fear he had harbored during his adult life had become reality.

Ross's story is bigger than one person, one family, one community, one hospital, and one disease. It spans many faith denominations. His life story was not about cancer, yet cancer was a major player in his life. He was first and foremost a dad. He was a husband, son, brother, grandson, nephew, and uncle. He was a trusted employee, a dedicated fireman, a master to his beagle, and a friend to many. He was a man of faith, which he demonstrated quietly in his love for others and care of creation. He lived as fully as he could in the time he was given. As he lived, he didn't consider himself a cancer survivor or victim.

UIHC and the Mayo Clinic are highly esteemed teaching hospi-tals. Over the course of Ross's forty-nine years, his life touched many students and improved medical research. He was part of many case studies. He was followed by the tumor registry at the University of Iowa Hospitals his entire life. He participated in studies, underwent many medical tests, answered many questions, was photographed in some of his most vulnerable moments, and always had a willing spirit when he could contribute to education. This was all part of the normal life he knew—at times when he was feeling well and during times of great suffering.

I read his autopsy report with a feeling of awe, realizing that this final report was a conclusion of decades of his medical records. At one time, we had pushed this same stack of records in a wheelchair down the halls of UIHC because it was so heavy.

November 2, 2010, was All Saints' Day, and once again, it was celebrated with tradition at our church. I did not participate as a worship leader for that service. I was sitting in a pew with my family as
the names were read of those who had passed away during the year.
With love and remembrance, candles were lit and a bell tolled during a moving communion service. Among those remembered: Ross
William Butterbrodt.

Words

WORDS ARE CENTRAL to our lives. Words are powerful. How frustrating it is when we're at a loss for words, and how often the perfect words come to us after a situation has passed. Sometimes words attract, and sometimes words repel. Sometimes words are just boring words. We build up and tear down with words. We hurt and heal with words. We learn to know the world through words, which, in the beginning, are not our own. Words influence our very being. Words create and give life meaning.

Finding one's own voice takes words. In much of life, all we have are words. We speak, read, and write with them. We converse, debate, teach, learn, remember, and dream. Our words express comfort, appreciation, agitation—the full range of human emotion—as well as ideas, insight, questions, and humor. Worship, prayer, and song are formed with words.

Words are bridges between human beings. Past, present, and future—words bridge the distance between an experience and its reliving. When a story is retold, it is relived.

Anais Nin said, "We write to taste life twice, in the moment and in retrospection." She also said, "We don't see things as they are, we see them as we are."[1]

This book is filled with my chosen words. Ross's experience birthed my writing. His choice of words would have been different from mine. This story is inspired by his life and death, using my words as a bridge from the past to the present. Unforgettable experiences were replayed in my mind, and grief was present as I wrote.

Ross was aware of the lasting impact he made on a multitude of lives. I told him there would be a book someday. He was so sick; he didn't care. To put it bluntly, this book didn't matter to him, but it's very important to me.

Many of my words are about a dying experience, but my words are also about life—born from deep moments of living. Read, hear, listen, and feel. It's not only about what is said but what is unsaid. Language can't do all the work. The spaces that yawn between words can be meaningful. There are certain events and experiences that defy the power of words, and emphasis is placed on the power of silence when words aren't necessary.

Prayers, relationships, hopes, and dreams are, thankfully, not fully dependent upon our ability to find words. A shared life gives words meaning. A communal story invites others to recognize themselves in it. You and I are a community. As I set my words carefully, one next to another, may they reach across our boundaries and bridge our distance. The right words can be a gift.

● ● ●

Quite often, I think about how many times things seem to go wrong. I also recognize when things seem right. I found author Kathleen Norris's writing just when I needed it, which was a true blessing for

---

1 "Popular Quotes," Goodreads, s.v. "Anais Nin," Accessed May 9, 2015, http://www.goodreads.com/quotes/.

me. During an earlier stretch of time when Ross's health was stable and our family life seemed predictable, her writing introduced me to the word *quotidian*, meaning "occurring every day, belonging to every day, commonplace, ordinary." Quotidian is *normal*. She taught me about finding holiness in ordinary, daily work. Her writing spoke to me during this normal time in my life.[2]

In ministry training, as I studied worship and the sacraments, the class had lively discussions about the church year, a majority of which is called ordinary time. This is the down time, between the *big* days—Christmas and Easter—and the meaningful seasons preceding them. Students were asked about their preferences for *ordinary* versus *big*, extraordinary times in the church year. Many students liked the extraordinary, feeling they ministered at their fullest during the periods from Advent to Christmas and from Lent to Easter. They were the people who said they liked surprise and unpredictability. They preferred action. They liked events.

Others of us preferred ordinary time—the daily grind, the times that speak of ritual, routine, and growth.

I crave ordinary. I crave stability, equilibrium, and a sense of balance, maybe even control—whether it's real or perceived. I can handle complexity, but I prefer a steady, somewhat predictable pace.

Quotidian is a great word, and I learned it at a time I call good. Through the years, there have been times when *normal* was far removed from my reality. I have a deep appreciation for the quotidian.

There was a time, in a hospital and environment far from home, when Ross's condition was teetering, and we were becoming further removed from quotidian life as we once knew it. I carried Kathleen's wisdom and experience with me as a companion. Thank you, Kathleen Norris.

• • •

2 Kathleen Norris, *The Quotidian Mysteries: Laundry, Liturgy and "Women's Work"* (Mahwah, NJ: Paulist Press, 1998).

I met the people who introduced me to words such as *radiation damage, friable tissue, borborygmi, duodenal jejunostomy, bacterial overgrowth, signet cell adenocarcinoma, rothia mucilaginosa*. They taught me a new language, face to face, when life wasn't normal. Their timing was perfect. The quotidian in those days was about life, stripped down to the basics: intake, output, breath, rest, and comfort. I was married to the person whose body was the complex organism that exemplified these words.

The Mayo Clinic and UIHC complemented one another with Ross's care. I will always be thankful for the wisdom gained from the exposure to and the insights of each institution. I recollect the communication, the expertise, the friendships, and the compassion that were demonstrated over a period of time that, in many ways, was the worst of times. There were doctors and nurses who accompanied us on the journey, and many of their words made a permanent imprint. There were occasions when I used their quotes in my journaling: the brief, direct quotes that summarized forward or backward progress with Ross's condition, the quotes that portrayed a feeling, or the quotes that served as markers of the time in which we lived. Sometimes strong statements like "It was tough, but Ross handled it," or "I never want to operate on him again" were simplified summaries of complex times.

• • •

It was December 2004; following a year in which Ross had been seriously ill, Mariah wrote the following words on Hello Kitty notepaper to her father:

Dear Dad, I hope you have a good Christmas this year. This is one we'll remember, right? I love you.—Ri.

The envelope was colored heavily with pink, purple, and green markers and included many hearts, a tree, and "Happy Holidays." She was nine years old. That was a Christmas we'll never forget. Ross had been hospitalized the better part of two months and was released from the hospital on Christmas Day. After returning home, he spent a lot of time crying, outwardly and inwardly.

There were many times when Mariah would say or write something—her words reminding me of the particular path we were on and also of the special bond of daughter and father—a bond that won't be matched or replaced.

Five years later, Mariah was in eighth grade, and Ross had his first surgery at Mayo. Because of her age, Mariah was not allowed in the Intensive Care Unit (ICU) after Ross's surgery. We took pictures of Ross and shared them with Mariah in the waiting room. After Ross was moved from the ICU to a regular hospital room, Mariah's age still prevented her from visiting. Only adults were permitted in the hospital due to a flu quarantine. She also had the sniffles. His surgery was November 9, 2009, and she did not get to see him until November 16. Those seven days were an eternity for both of them, and she concocted many ideas about how she could get into the hospital. She posted the following message online:

> *Yes, Mom. I can pass for 18. I will wear some high heels and stuff and I will put on a lot of makeup to look like I'm 18. Don't worry! Love You!!! Mariah*☺

During some stressful and worrisome days, Mariah's words provided us with welcome comic relief. She couldn't fathom the concepts behind open-backed hospital gowns, portable shampoo stations, and infrequent showers for critically ill patients. She would make us laugh.

• • •

With the thrill of hope, a weary world rejoices. It was Christmas Eve 2009 and ups and downs continued. We were cautiously optimistic and hopefully realistic. Joyful melancholy filled us. I wrote the following prayer for the candlelight worship service:

> *God of all time, we retell the Christmas story, once again. We wait eagerly for the birth of the Promised One who turns the darkness into light, and in his birth brings eternal hope. It's Christmas Eve. We give you thanks, and we know that the Lord will come. We thank you for pouring out your life into the human form of Jesus and for the continual rebirth of Christ in the human heart. May the joy of Christmas never end but continue through the ages until, at last, your reign of justice and peace is fully established on this earth. On this night, O God, we pray that your love surround those in need, those who are suffering in mind, body, or spirit. Grant strength and comfort to those who are healing, to those who are ill, lonely, anxious, or doubting. Watch over those who are working this night for our safety and protection. We pray that each of us here will safely arrive at the places where we will celebrate Christmas, and may our celebrations be filled with what is longed for—whether it be peace and stillness, or excitement and energy. Fill our lives, O God, as we pray in the name of Jesus, the Christ. Amen.*

Life was perpetual prayer in those days, a prayer alive with care and compassion. Each conversation seemed to be filled with prayer, and every encounter seemed sacred. Sometimes there weren't words, but there was prayerful, heartfelt communication in touch, expression, gesture, and breath. The bodies that surrounded Ross's sick body carried the message.

There were many days when I wore my stress. Late one night on a shuttle from the hospital to my hotel, the driver looked at me and said, "When I run out of words to pray, my prayer is always for peace." I scribbled his words in my journal, and acknowledged there was wisdom and care surrounding me in all places.

Sometimes the only words of prayer I could muster were "Hold me, God."

Ross wasn't always in favor of praying. He had a strong faith, and he wrestled with it. In palliative care, the only outward expression of Ross's faith was his response to the Lord's Prayer. He liked that prayer, prayed slowly. There were times when these familiar prayerful words were the only ones I could rally as we marked time. I was thankful for those words.

I wrestled with my dual roles of spouse and pastor. I felt guilty for my ability to minister to strangers while feeling inadequate ministering to my husband. I would vent my frustrations to Ross and then feel selfish. I was envious of people whose lives seemed normal. I resolved that I would live the role of caregiver to its fullest. To me caregiver was an accomplished blend of spouse and pastor. I gained an appreciation for folks who can achieve their professional roles with family members.

I now realize the role I executed fully was that of a human being doing what was necessary at the time.

• • •

In a previous decade or my other life, I attended a seminar led by Willard "Sandy" Boyd, president emeritus of the University of Iowa. His agenda was businesslike in nature, but his fascinating persona and his exceptional speaking ability shone through. The topic was gratitude. Often he referred to being "in praise of praise" and the importance of two words: *thank you*. His philosophy was that these two words are necessary and need to be said a lot. He suggested that gratitude blesses both giver and receiver. People are so busy, rushing to get places and to get everything done. Gratitude slows us down, and appreciation and acknowledgement take time and thought. Time is a rare commodity. Taking things for granted reflects being comfortable in the familiar. Being comfortable can be good. We need to be comfortable but not at the expense of forgetting our *thank-yous*.

I agree with Willard Boyd. In April 2010 I was the recipient of the following note:

> *Dear Mom,*
>
> *I love you! Thank you for being my mom! You have done a lot for me in my 14 years of life. I appreciate everything you do for me, even though sometimes I don't show it. Thanks! I don't say that a lot but inside I do! Thank you for everything you do for me! You are the best mom! You do a lot for our family. It is so nice for how much you help Dad. It has been crazy but good. Thank you very much!*
>
> *Love, Mariah*

What had become familiar to us was not comfortable, but we had proven to be adaptable to the unease life had handed us. And I had children who remembered to express gratitude. Thank God.

The doctor from UIHC who knew Ross best shared some of his wisdom with us. We will be perpetually grateful for his words:

> *Fairness is a concept that humans invented to deal with each other, it is not a property of the universe. It is normal to be depressed in a depressing situation. There is supposedly an art to accepting the things you can't change, but I can't say I have mastered it. Some anger and frustration may be a good thing. Situations such as yours create gallows humor. It is like the joke*

among combat veterans: When it really hurts after you get shot, at least it means you are still alive. Focus on those good things we all have every day.

As I write, I experience a part of my life again. In retrospect,

"Something sinister is going on in Ross's abdomen," said the surgeon.
"Your case is very complex," said the oncologist.
"This isn't going to end well," said Ross.
"It will all be okay, Mother," said Devin.

Hopes and Dreams

THE WORD *HAPPY* is an adjective I use with care. To me, the word is somewhat superficial and overused. There are many other words that seem more accurately descriptive: *joyful, elated, untroubled, delighted, pleased,* and *gratified* are all great words. However, there are times when *happy* is the suitable word to use.

As I read through my writing of hopes and dreams in my children's baby books, I come across the word *happy* quite frequently. During my pregnancies and the first months and years of my children's lives, it was my wish that their lives be filled with happiness, confidence, and contentment, and it's still my wish even now that they are grown. *Happy* seems to be an appropriate word when dreaming about a child's future. It is obvious that my parents and Ross's parents dreamed, and still dream, of happiness and contentment for their children, grandchildren, and future generations—just as their parents dreamed for them.

Dreams for loved ones never include illness, poor health, brokenness, fear, or an uncertain future. These situations breed unhappiness. In reality, these situations occur. I cannot imagine the feelings of helplessness and unhappiness that parents of a critically ill child have. Sadness, fear, uncertainty, and exhaustion consumed the household during Ross's childhood cancer diagnosis and treatment.

My heart goes out to his parents and all who were significant in those early years of his difficult health journey. Through the years when I was his primary caregiver, I thought a lot about how life must have been in those early years, when cancer survival was rare.

I think about the hopes and dreams of my parents for me. I know there have been times when my reality has not been close to anything my parents dreamed of or hoped for me. I also know that times of great difficulty and adversity can contribute to growth in ways that can only be learned by experience. Experience shapes life.

Henry J. Harwick, Mayo's first chief of administration, wrote about the difficulty the Mayo Clinic faced during the depression years. He wrote of his "conviction that often out of bad may come something enduringly good." He states, "Adversity at any time, if faced up to and beaten, is not at all a bad thing; among other rewards, one gains in wisdom for the very good reason that one must survive."[3]

When Ross was a palliative care patient, reflective, intense, and emotional discussions took place in the decision-making processes involved with his care. In a conversation two weeks prior to his death, Ross was asked of his hopes and dreams for the rest of his life. Ross answered, "Dreams for the rest of my life have been shattered." His plain, simple, and true words left the social worker silent and caused tears to sting my eyes and roll down my cheeks. Shattered dreams—I have reflected upon this profound statement multiple times. I hear it as spouse, parent, child, and widow. Like glass breaking on a tile floor, the fragments of one person's broken dreams splinter through many lives, affecting the multiple roles of each person.

Upon hearing Ross's words, I knew there would be many shards of broken dreams scattered throughout our lives, to be discovered at different times in the future. My children no longer dream of a future that

---

3   Henry J. Harwick, *Forty-Four Years with the Mayo Clinic: 1908–1952* (Rochester, MN: Mayo Foundation for Medical Education and Research, 2012), 27.

includes their father's physical presence. Ross's parents' dreams for their son ended but carry on for the generations that follow. As I dream about my future, there is uncertainty. My parents' dreams have changed.

In all the sadness and reshaping of life, I've observed that we are still dreamers. We look to the future and wonder what will unfold. I hear my children talk about their aspirations for the future. We are still living.

One week prior to his death, Ross said, "I'm not going home, am I?"

I said, "No. Is there anything you want?"

He said, "I would like to see Chassis once more."

Chassis (pronounced "Chassie"—like the car part for which she was named) was our then two-year-old beagle. Chassis was *the* dog that Ross had dreamed about for years before I was finally convinced that we *needed* a dog. Ross was Chassis's master and best friend. She listened to him, comforted him, stayed close by him, and gave him so much joy. *Happy* is an appropriate word to use when referring to the feeling Chassis gave Ross.

Seeing Chassis one more time was the fulfillment of Ross's final dream. Chas was brought to Iowa City and met us in the garden in front of the hospital. Our kids were there, and it was as sweet as sweet could be. Ross's good-bye to Chassis was heartbreaking and very, very special. It was on that day, in that place, that our last and most treasured family picture was taken. That was the last time the five of us, plus the dog, were together. That evening, I wrote the following entry to our friends in my online journal:

> *The kids have gone home...to live. They have endured so much in the past year, and now Ross and I request that they do not sit and endure this wait. We are all at peace with one another—sad, but at peace. And now I sit in a darkened, quiet room with Ross. I want it this way. You have been with us on this journey, but nobody can know what it has been to live it. His experience*

has consumed me to the fullest and has forever changed every aspect of my life.

For the past six years, I have been Ross's caregiver. Since November 2009, that role has been at a very intense level. For the past twenty-seven years, I have been Ross's wife. During intense times of caregiving, it is impossible to fulfill all expectations of spouse and caregiver, as well as mother, daughter, sister, aunt, granddaughter, niece, friend, and pastor. Caregiver was the hat I had to wear, and we owe so many thanks to everyone who allowed me to perform that role.

Now I have been relieved of my caregiving duties. (The nurses say I'm supervising.) I am Ross's wife and Devin, Randy, and Mariah's mom. I am where I need to be, and my final measure of care for my husband is to give him a well-deserved peaceful, quiet, pain-free, and worry-free death.

In the past months, so much seemed to continually go wrong. This part will go right and work in Ross's favor. We know, without a doubt, what he's guaranteed and what we're all guaranteed.

As I reread these words, I realize they summarize a dream of death. I also realize the questions that are embedded in them. How will I change? How will the kids and I heal? Will my faith falter?

Earlier I had written of my hope that Ross die at night with only me there, that he could say all the proper good-byes, and that all the necessary good-byes could be said to him. I wondered how he would handle his good-byes, and I concluded that he would do it in his simple, profound way. I wrote:

I really do hope he dies quietly, at night—in front of nobody but me. I think that's what he will want too. And I will thank God the following morning—that he didn't have to struggle one more night. Life will be different that day when the sun comes up.

Not every dream comes true, but that one did.

• • •

Vaclav Havel in *Disturbing the Peace* says,

> *Hope is a state of mind, not a state of the world. Either we have hope within us or we don't; it is a dimension of the soul, and it's not essentially dependent on some particular observation of the world or estimate of the situation. Hope is not prognostication. It is an orientation of the spirit, an orientation of the heart; it transcends the world that is immediately experienced, and is anchored somewhere beyond its horizons...Hope, in this deep and powerful sense, is not the same as joy that things are going well, or willingness to invest in enterprises that are obviously heading for early success, but, rather, an ability to work for something because it is good, not just because it stands a chance to succeed. The more propitious the situation in which we demonstrate hope, the deeper that hope is. Hope is definitely not the same thing as optimism. It is not the conviction that something will turn out well, but the certainty that something makes sense regardless of how it turns out.[4]*

Hope in the face of death is very different from hope in the face of life. I continually relied on my faith and the definition of hope that Christianity provides: the hope of eternal life. There were times when I was blind to hope in the earthly, human sense. There are times it's good we can't know the future, but we can cling to hope as defined by Mr. Havel.

In my role as pastor, I faced situations of sudden, unforeseen death. With unexpected death often come words such as *If only I would have known* and *I would have done things differently.*

---

4   Vaclav Havel, *Disturbing the Peace* (New York: Alfred A. Knopf, 1990), 181.

I vividly remember these words resounding once when a prominent church member had suddenly passed away. *If only we would have known.* The words prompted a dream for me, a real, *in-my-sleep* dream. I dreamed I was with a large group of women in the church kitchen, all of us knowing that the death of this church member was going to take place. The person was there but didn't know she was going to die. None of us assembled knew how to live with our knowledge of her upcoming death. We treated her differently, not knowing how to interact with one another or with her, because we knew. We were afraid. It became nightmarish, and the dream ended when I awakened, startled and confused.

Following Ross's death, I had many startling dreams and nightmares. A slow process of death has ugly physical elements, and I remember some stuff from his last days being fodder for nightmares. I had a recurring nightmare of him vomiting on me. This had happened in real life, but it was never as intense as in the nightmare. Months after his funeral, I had a dream he was alive in his casket during his funeral and we patiently waited at the cemetery for his death before the burial took place.

These visions, dreams, and nightmares contributed to real-life exhaustion. I faced sleep with apprehension. I dreamed of the day when the nightmares would end. They did, but I think about those dreams and nightmares from time to time. It's good we have this subconscious outlet to process our innermost and guarded thoughts and emotions. It may be to our advantage not to know everything about when death will come. Instead, it's good to live with a consciousness that does not dwell on death but aspires to hope—hope beyond human understanding.

Cancer

MARIAH SAID, "SO, that means Dad will have cancer for the rest of his life."

I said, "Yes."

As a young adult and person with a history of cancer, Ross had been invited to participate in studies through the UIHC tumor-registry program. He had agreed, with hesitation. Would cancer be revealed in any of the studies? He had worried.

One study had consisted of a fertility test. The results had indicated the unlikelihood that Ross's sperm would ever penetrate an egg. In all probability, the radiation he had received as a child had made him sterile. When this news circulated, I recall his Grandma Velma encouraging us to keep an open mind about adoption. I made peace with the possibility of never bearing children. Ross is the father of our children. There are three miracles in this story.

Ross had a hernia and hydrocele repair procedure in 1985. He was terrified that cancer would be revealed. No cancer.

There were many times when Ross had panic attacks. Anxiety about cancer was at the root of these attacks. Sometimes he'd focus on a mole, sometimes a cough following a cold, and sometimes it was just an unsettled feeling. Ross would jump to the conclusion that he had cancer. I know this fear is common for folks we call cancer

survivors. His anxiety and depression were controlled with medication. His medication was monitored closely and constantly tweaked.
However, there isn't medication that can eradicate the fear of cancer.

Between 1989 and 2009, Ross had numerous surgeries and ail-
ments due to the effects of his cancer treatment in the 1960s.
Foremost in his mind each time was the threat of cancer's return. He
endured a lot in these years, but no health issues were attached to a
cancer diagnosis even though he worried.

Early in 2010 while he was being treated for complicated digestive problems, there was a thyroid-cancer scare. Tests were pointing to the chance that Ross had thyroid cancer. We held our breath.
After an exasperating winter of illness, we couldn't fathom adding
cancer to the equation. We were braced to receive bad news, but the
biopsy was clear. No cancer. We exhaled and went on with caring for
his many and varied health problems.

I was by Ross's side during all of the imagined and real cancer scares
in his adult life. Each time, I could not escape these thoughts: *What if?
What would his reaction be? What would my reaction be? Where would
it lead?* I had practice with wrapping my head around the concept of
cancer. Or at least I thought I did. When cancer was real, it was different than I imagined. Preconceived notions about what our actions
and reactions might be dissipated with Ross's cancer diagnosis.

Every cancer journey forges new territory. Uncharted, life-changing paths are traveled. Along the way, valuable knowledge, deepened
faith, cherished memories, and scars are among the "souvenirs." The
raw experience of cancer interrupted and invaded our lives for only a
few months but with a vengeance.

Ross had been healing slowly, often stagnating or moving backward, following complications of his major surgery in November 2009.
He was miserable, and I was completely overwhelmed. The month of
May 2010 was a short reprieve, but he moved into June with flare-ups
of old symptoms at their worst and new symptoms that caused many
heads to spin.

On June 4, Ross was having difficulty breathing. This was new. A specialized lung x-ray at UIHC preceded another emergent trip to Mayo. He was admitted to Saint Mary's Hospital in Rochester, and his symptoms multiplied: a cough, more shortness of breath, a new tiredness, and different chest sounds. He was diagnosed with a pleural effusion, meaning the pleura or casing around the right lung was filled with fluid. This decreased his lung capacity and was cause for more testing as well as tapping (draining) his lung.

The cytology report of the tapped lung was clear, and he was sent home when it seemed safe. Within days there were signs of fluid reaccumulation, and we found ourselves back at the UIHC emergency room. Deep concerns entered the picture. Testing on that day revealed tumor activity. Ross became very sick, very quickly. UIHC wanted to transport Ross to Mayo via ambulance; however, Ross refused. My car was once again the medical transport. We left on my promise not to stop until we got to Saint Mary's. By the grace of God, we arrived safely.

Upon Ross's readmittance to Saint Mary's, more pleural fluid was drained, as well as fluid that had accumulated in his abdominal cavity. An image-guided needle biopsy followed. It was a time of extreme pain, long tests, and compounded worries. All of this was in addition to his postsurgical and digestive-tract discomforts.

The sense of impending doom heightened. The words *breathe in, breathe out* took on deeper meaning as Ross worked hard to breathe, and I found myself holding my own breath in suspense. When all tests were completed and all necessary specimens collected, including removal of a fast-growing mole on his chin, we were informed that preliminary results could take twenty-four hours and final reports as long as three to five days. We took it one step at a time as the pieces were analyzed and put together. A catheter was surgically placed for draining Ross's right lung.

Cancer was the enemy cloud that loomed.

In my church work, I'd been in this place with other folks, but our own situation was nearly more than I could bear. An identity crisis was my affliction. I didn't feel strong or pastoral.

It was during this time of extreme anxiety that we met Patrick, one of Ross's nurses, who will be remembered with admiration. Patrick's care was exemplary, and the friendship that developed between the two men was immediate. Patrick was a farm boy at heart. Farming, fishing, biking, and golfing stories were shared. Patrick could provide lightness to Ross's heavy days. I could rest at night knowing Ross was in Patrick's care.

Ross's preliminary cancer diagnosis came on June 14, 2010. There was a mass growing on the exterior surface of his kidney. There were probably more tumors, possibly related to his childhood cancer or radiation damage. The news we received did not sound hopeful. On June 15 I wrote:

We are in shock but trying to stabilize following the cancer news and painful catheter experiences. Patrick has joined our journey, and in a very short time, he has moved up high on Ross's list of favorites. Patrick is a farm boy, so there is much to talk about. Ross says that Patrick stands next to medical equipment—IV poles, PCA pumps—like he's leaning on a fence post. Patrick says that's what he intends it to look like. Patrick has capable hands. He emits trustworthiness. He's met his calling. Everybody loves Patrick, and Patrick seems to love everybody. He's one example of the excellence that surrounds us. While we feel far away from home and miss everyone like crazy, we're walking on holy ground here. This is where Ross needs to be.

Ross's doctors are experts, not only in their fields but also in compassion. Confidence radiates from them, and we're assured they will find some answers to the ever-growing list of questions. The complete diagnosis will take time, but it's necessary

*as they lay groundwork for a plan. They are studying all of Ross's
records, dating back to the 1960s, looking for insight, taking one
step at a time, and recognizing the importance of being patient
with the process.*

*The cancer news was shared with Devin, Randy, and Mariah.
It was shared with our parents who shared it with extended family and friends. There are many sad people. God's taking care of
us all, because that's what God does. We're in God's hands.*

We knew Ross had cancer, but there was more to be determined. It
would take time. The waiting place was in the hospital. The waiting
place was at the hotel. The waiting place was a deep, dark place inside
us, everywhere we were. We waited in Rochester, and a community
waited at home. Patrick waited with us. What would final reports
reveal? Again, a trip to Rochester turned from days to weeks. I saw
the doctors and the hotel staff more than I saw my children.

In this time of extreme anxiety, there were experiences that
held buffer-like qualities, for which I was grateful. The kids came to
Rochester as often as possible, gracing us with not only their presence but also smiles and laughter. Their visits would be greatly anticipated but often would not go as we hoped. Ross's condition was not
always conducive to quality conversation or activity. Sometimes he
could tolerate visitors and sometimes not. We would leave Ross rest-
ing and escape to our sanctuary, the Honker. There was great importance in being together, even though heartbreak and disappointment
were involved. The coziness of my hotel room felt like a safety net.

Inside the hospital was one world, and outside the hospital was
another. Each world was real, but it was hard to determine what was
normal. Had we entered middle-earth? The answer could be debated.
Imagining the experience and living this reality were two different
things.

Weather affected us very little, yet we were aware of extreme
weather conditions from inside the hospital room. Heat indexes of

104 degrees led to raging storms with crashing thunder, vivid light-ning, and torrential rain. Then the sun would come out, even as Canadian wildfires hazed Rochester with a fog. The air had a scent of burning pine. It was like cancer in the atmosphere.

Storms raged inside Ross's body too. He became sicker: vomiting, diarrhea, abdominal discomfort, dehydration, swelling, debilitating headaches, and difficulty breathing. So much was unknown, and the big question was, how much time did he have? A stent was surgically inserted in his intestine, which was nearly 100 percent blocked. This was an act of desperation intended to give some relief to a digestive system not only rampant with cancer but with bacterial overgrowth and infection. Veins in Ross's arms were being destroyed from all the needles. It was setback after setback as we trudged, feeling drowned, in this journey. Ross's internal storms would sometimes lessen for short reprieves: sometimes minutes, sometimes hours, but never longer. This would ease the mental anguish temporarily. A point of stability wasn't attainable.

Doctors were trying with all their might to keep him comfortable, nourished, hydrated, and rested, as well as to keep his depression at bay. At the same time, they were at work to determine the type of cancer cells that had invaded his body and the location of the pri-mary tumor. Various procedures and numerous tests often resulted in more questions. They pored through his medical records. Nutrition was complicated, and comfort required drugs. There was a point when it appeared that he had two cancers, which was mind-boggling. The presentation and composition of his cancer were not typical, which caused the experts to restudy everything in order to prescribe a treatment. We were told there were seven oncologists working on his case, and Ross was becoming well known in Mayo oncology. That made Ross feel confident in his team and their decisions, but he hated that his case needed special attention. He was often referred to as *special, rare,* and *peculiar.* Thankfully, he could find smiles and humor in some dreadful situations.

Throughout everything, Ross only complained to me. There was a lot he could have complained about but didn't. As bad as he felt—sometimes much worse than other times—anyone could walk in the room and ask how he was, and 99 percent of the time his answer was, "Good." All of his nurses commented about this. They were used to dealing with complainers.

Riveting processes and discussions happened. I could see the difficulty of Ross's situation in the eyes of his doctors. I went to bed each night with information overload. A lot was in flux, yet the consistency of the compassion that surrounded us never wavered. The compassion of Ross's team felt like the glue that kept us from coming undone.

A unique relationship develops between patient, doctor, and family. I witnessed this between the sickest of the sick in patients and the best of the best in doctors. I admired the many ways doctors cared for Ross while also attending to the questions and anxiety the kids and I had. For those who have never experienced this relationship—congratulations. You are fortunate. For those who know about the relationship to which I refer, you understand the rapport that develops with the professionals who care for you. Whatever the serious condition that caused the relationship, the bond that develops becomes one of the largest of life's blessings. In all of Ross's distress, he was blessed over and over with these bonds. He cherished them, esteemed them, and held them close. For Ross, his list of favorite people included several doctor friends.

Cancer is a big diagnosis is a combination of words I never forgot as Ross's cancer story began unfolding, and we began learning a new language—words strung together about cells, studies, reports, and tumor activity. There were so many questions, and experts advised us not to wonder but just to wait for results. These are wise words of advice but are challenging to follow. Life seemed to unravel and quickly spiral downward. We were missing what we used to call normal, and the word *quotidian* took on new meaning.

Finally, the complete pathology report was posted: signet cell adenocarcinoma. After all the lab work, discussion, and study, the experts were certain his cancer had begun in his colon and metastasized. One cancer was at work in his body, running rampant. We considered this to be good bad news, the good being that we finally had the full diagnosis.

The next day's journal entry dealt with the question "How is Ross?" It read as follows:

Most of his time is spent being physically miserable. There are moments when he feels okay. Thank God for those moments. There have been overwhelming amounts of information to hear and diagnoses that are nearly impossible to comprehend. Pardon the pun, but there is way too much to digest. Most of his energy is spent physically, and we can only speculate about what it must be like to be him, physically and mentally, right now.

As much as Ross likes to talk, he does not talk much about how he feels. He would rather talk about cars and trucks, selling livestock feed, the fire department, baseball, crops, weather, and of course Devin, Randy, Mariah, and Chassis. Conversation seems to be a much-needed buffer, when he's up to it. When he decides to say more, what he shares is profound. As dire as the situation is, he has not given up. Comfort is of utmost importance, and when he's comfortable, his spirits are pretty good.

Here are two short examples that say a lot about how Ross is:

Yesterday, his favorite Mayo doctor walked in and asked, "How are you?" Ross's simple answer was "I wish I wasn't laying here in this condition." That sums it up.

Yesterday, when the final cancer diagnosis was given, the doctors appeared to be prepared for a bigger reaction than they got. We had a room full of professionals with us. Nobody wanted to be there, but believe it or not, the conversation was rather uneventful considering the seriousness. When the room

had cleared, I asked Ross, "How are you?" His answer was "Sad."
Within a minute he was sound asleep and snoring. Sad is the
short, but complete, summary of how Ross is feeling.

Ross was not a candidate for surgery or radiation, so a chemo plan was formulated. A variation of FOLFOX chemotherapy would be used. The best that could be hoped for was to shrink the tumor sites by 25 percent. There was a 10–40 percent chance of this happening. The outlook was bleak, and the risks of chemo could be deadly. Ross was dehydrated and malnourished. A person should be stronger to begin chemo, but his condition was balanced with risks of waiting. Ross made the decision to begin the necessary clearance steps and start immediately. His requests were honored in all of his care. The control attached to this was immeasurable for him. There were times when his choices were life-versus-death decisions. Plans were made to move Ross from Saint Mary's medical unit to the oncology unit at Rochester Methodist Hospital.

On July 12, he was transported by Mayo's Gold Cross Ambulance Service from hospital to hospital. During Ross's hyperbaric-oxygen treatments in November, we had become familiar with the ambulance system and staff. The medical technicians and I exchanged not only small talk but also things like recipes and advice. This hospital-to-hospital transport was a reunion of sorts with ambulance friends.

We arrived at Rochester Methodist Hospital, Station 44, Room 4-407 in the afternoon. Ross was exhausted, in pain, nauseated, emotional, and swollen. His words were "I'm a mess."

He was transferred from gurney to hospital bed, met his nurse, settled for a minute, and then he needed to use the restroom. Moving him with IV pole, tubes, and all of his swelling and discomfort wasn't easy, but it was accomplished with expertise. I tried my best to allow the whole process to work without my intervention. I was also exhausted, so I sat down, looking out the window at a new view. Ross was on the toilet. The nurse stepped out to retrieve more paperwork.

For a moment, I looked around and realized how noticeably different the oncology ward atmosphere was in comparison to the medical ward where Ross had been. It was different in a serious, cancer-oriented way. The walls breathed of treatment sights and sounds. There was a definite feeling of unity as every patient had cancer. Everyone who works there knows cancer. Cancer is the specialty.

My thoughts were interrupted by the sound of running water. But it wasn't water; it was the sound of urine hitting the bathroom floor. At first, Ross didn't realize he was peeing on his pants and the floor. When Ross realized what he was doing, he said, "It's hard to pee in the toilet when your nuts are the size of grapefruits." He kicked off his pants and socks. The nurse cleaned it up. No worries—they're used to this stuff.

At that same moment, another nurse popped in and said the guitar-playing music therapist was in the hallway and asked if it was okay if he played music outside Ross's door. Ross rolled his eyes but agreed. As the nurse scrubbed and helped Ross change, the guitar playing began. The volume escalated, as did the animation of the performer. I saw dancing in my peripheral vision. The phone rang. It was Ross's surgeon calling to check in. I couldn't hear him. The music was loud. There was commotion all around, and then the oncology team walked in the door. It was nightmarish. There were tears welling up in my tired, tired eyes. My only thought at that very moment was *This is cancer.*

• • •

I was continually asked why Ross's cancer wasn't found earlier. The answer was that it wasn't there to be found. There was no trace when he had complete scans in December or any tests after that. Nothing indicated cancer. The day of diagnosis, I asked the oncologist how long he thought the cancer had been growing. The answer was "Maybe a few weeks." It was an aggressive cancer. As we thought back to the end of May, we remembered that forward progress had seemed to go backward. This could have been the onset. The likelihood that Ross's tissue had been harboring cancer for forty-seven years was high. Ross was facing the situation he had worried about for decades. Cancer was threatening his life.

We held our breath as chemotherapy began. His first treatment was rather uneventful. He was an inpatient and monitored closely, so minor incidents with an IV line, some tingling, and his potassium levels were all handled as they happened. In the forty-eight hours he was receiving chemo, his eyes were brighter and his mind clearer than they had been for a while. I remembered being puzzled by this, but the experts said it's often the case. I learned lessons about toxicity as we added that concept to our life in a new way.

The first round of chemo ended and so did the short spell of bright eyes and clear mind. Two units of blood were infused because Ross's hemoglobin dropped to 7.5. This number was about half of what it should have been. More serious discussions took place, and his team continued to watch and check all the things that needed to be watched and checked.

We learned about "chemo fog" and "chemo tired." Just as there is no pain like cancer's pain, there is no tired that can be compared to chemo tired. Ross was placed in the expert category of these topics by all of us who surrounded him.

His vomit changed in consistency, and it was suspected he was vomiting pieces of tumor. I clearly remember that day and other similar times when I thought, *I can't believe this is happening.*

• • •

Our hometown community was planning a benefit for Ross, and that date was approaching. Yellow and orange wristbands were being sold. They became widely known as "Ross bracelets." Mariah helped design them. They had a fire department logo and "Ross" inscribed in them. Most people we knew were wearing one of each color. Mariah said they kept the bracelets plain and simple because Ross was plain and simple. His medical team and I did not agree with her statement. Had they asked for Ross's input about the bracelet inscription, he would have said to print "Shit happens." Many of his doctors and nurses sported these bracelets on their wrists. That was humbling.

One day, during a time when Ross was wakeful and unhooked from the IV pole, I took him outside in his wheelchair. We were in a garden area outside of Rochester Methodist Hospital. Heavy, humid, hot air felt great to him after breathing dry hospital air. I'm not sure anyone else felt joy in breathing outside at the time. We sat in the garden, and a butterfly landed on Ross's lap. We watched it for a long time. He stated that one had landed on him the last time he was outside too. I told him that his hospital gown must look like a big blue flower to the butterfly. I remember sitting there looking at the butterfly, thinking, *I wonder if butterflies get cancer.*

This is an example of a time when it occurred to me how these days were different from what I knew as normal. In the old normal, there would not be time to stare at a butterfly. There were too many things to do in a day. I'm not sure Ross ever really noticed butterflies before. This peaceful experience didn't last long. He vomited and was overcome by pain as soon as we returned to his hospital room.

People from home heard this story, and in no time, butterflies became an icon for Ross. T-shirts were printed. The design included butterflies and the words *Ross's journey of hope.* Things like this happen when cancer is involved.

I don't know what it's like to have cancer, but I learned a lot by observation, and I knew about caregiving. I've witnessed many brave souls. There were moments each day when these words passed through my mind: *This is cancer.*

Cancer treatment complicates every medical issue. Cancer is as individual as a person is, and it's very unpredictable. Cancer even gets blamed for things that aren't related to cancer.

Cancer plays mind games and body games. It can make you feel strong, and it can make you feel weak. Obviously, it causes the worst of times, but it can also bring out some of the best gifts that humans have to offer. Cancer is the least desirable thing that thrives in or on the human body, yet it is a part of each human that it touches. Sometimes cancer becomes bigger than it deserves to be. Even the word sounds undesirable.

Cancer affects individuals, families, and communities. There are times when it can build up and times when it can tear down. It digs up the past and messes with the future. It is the source of much worry, and it hurts so badly. There is no pain like cancer pain.

Cancer is surrounded by information, yet there is so much unknown about it. Some yearn for information, and some prefer the power of denial as they cope. It is a reason for careers and success and a reason for sadness. Some even associate cancer with failure. It has created strategies for coping: slogans, icons, colors. It has created businesses and charities and educational opportunities. It's the topic of books, conversations, prayers, and poems, yet sometimes there aren't words to deal with it. This is cancer.

On a typical day, I would arrive at the hospital to catch puke and observe pain, suffering, extreme tiredness, uncertainty, and sadness. Yet sometimes I observed and celebrated easier breathing. I also heard some laughter and stories and visited with some of the best experts. Medical and oncology issues continued to make the experts scratch their heads. Stability was nearly impossible. Nothing went uninvestigated or assumed. This was all in Ross's room but not just in Ross's room. It was in every room in Station 44. Because this is cancer.

Early morning was usually rough. Sometimes there would be some improvement to his comfort as the day progressed. Plans were constantly being adapted and changed, depending on his various issues such as infections, swelling, breathing difficulties, and more.

What caused what? There were many mysteries. Some were solved and some weren't. Because this is cancer.

Symptoms would sneak back with the night. Patterns developed and so did methods for dealing with the symptoms. Ross's body was on overload, and his concentration was very physical. My mind was on overload, and my concentration was very mental. We were missing home in very physical and mental ways. The people in our various circles were being great as cancer ran the show.

• • •

There are things in life we take for granted. Think about taking a shower. For a large part of the world, water supply is a problem. But in the United States, we tend to take things like safe, running water for granted. We take for granted the mere luxury of having a shower and a paid water bill. For many of us, we can take a shower without thinking about it.

For a seriously ill person, a shower is a major undertaking. It was that way for Ross. The preparation consisted of unhooking and capping tubes, wrapping his torso in plastic, and keeping incisions, drain tubes, and catheters covered and dry. He had to sit for showers, as it took too much energy for him to stand. He would tremble and pant the entire time. He seemed to decline physically with each shower. When a shower was over, the process was reversed. Shaking and short of breath, he would have to be dried, unwrapped, dressed, and reconnected to everything. Then he would be put to bed and need to recover—from a shower. He couldn't shave and shower at the same time. It was too taxing. Brushing his teeth took energy he didn't have. Bed to bathroom was often the only walking he was able to do. It was heartbreaking. Heartbreak was normal.

One day, in a state of heartbreak, I fled the hospital for a pick-me-up haircut. I needed to feel better, and my spirit needed a lift. It didn't work out so well, as I received the worst haircut of my life. I should have opted for Bunnie cake instead.

I had been on antidepressants for quite some time. In October 2009 Ross's antidepressant medication had been increased, and I was encouraged to consider getting a prescription for myself. I heeded this advice and was thankful I did. At the time, we anticipated a difficult journey. That was before cancer.

After cancer entered the picture, I wasn't the only one taking a prescription. Anxiety and indigestion treatment worked its way into the family circle. Cancer can tear other bodies apart too. It continually amazed me how simultaneously strong yet fragile the human body is.

Ross lived with cancer, and we lived with Ross. Time inched along. Life was being lived day by day, and we learned about trust in new ways. Sometimes it was as if we didn't know how to be, but good days were the goal as each today became a tomorrow and our future unfolded.

People told me I was living in hell. They said this meaning to acknowledge the dreadful situation in which we lived. I disagreed—not about our dreadful situation, but about hell.

I could never say it was hell. I thought a lot about how the world defines *hell* and came to my own conclusion that hell is separation from God. Never did I feel separated from God. Therefore, never did I live in hell.

Through my years in ministry, and during Ross's illness, I heard a lot and read a lot about God and cancer. Many of those words made me cringe, but they also made me think. These are the things I believe:

- Don't blame God for cancer or say God gave it to us.
- We believe in a God who is good. A good God doesn't do this. A good God is with us in the worst of times.
- Cancer isn't punishment.

- Cancer is part of a person; it is produced in a body and thrives on the very things that feed the healthy parts of a body.
- Regardless of cancer's type or size, I agree with the doctor. *Cancer is a big diagnosis.*

I was often confused about the power of positive thinking. There *was* a power at work, but it came from realistic thinking. The UIHC doctor closest to Ross said these words to us: "It's okay to be negative. You have every reason to be negative. There is no proven research that positive or negative thoughts have any effect on tumors."

I will be ever thankful for his words that gave us permission to be negative.

As more unraveling took place, Ross often placed himself in a state of nonreality. It bothered me and the kids to know he was dying and yet listen to him make plans for what we'd do as a family in the future, babbling on as if nothing were wrong. He talked about attending Devin's college graduation. He talked about going to Chicago for a Cub's game. He talked about mixing feed rations for farm animals. Cancer was messing with his mind, and his words were messing with us.

I wanted him to talk about dying, to face his mortality, and see this time as an opportunity to teach the world, or at least our children, great things. I was temporarily blind to what he had taught us throughout his illnesses, blind to the profound wisdom he had shared, and blind to the bravery he had shown. One of the "best of the best" doctors called him valiant.

My blindfold was removed, but I was losing focus, finding myself overly concerned that Ross's sense of false hope would prove destructive in some way. Panic was snowballing in me. I must have been showing it when my burden was lifted. One of the experts gave me a new perspective for dealing with Ross's nonreality. She said, "Go there with him." The kids and I were given permission to meet him where he was. These words were one of the greatest gifts I have ever received.

We had permission to be negative and permission to pretend. There was a bittersweet shift. Ross's nonreality was a coping mechanism for him. As long as the kids and I were living with realistic views, there was no danger for us to pretend with Ross. He was dreaming of a future that wouldn't be, but it was better than his present reality. His reality sucked.

Cancer sucks.

Fear

WHEN OUR SON Randy was a young boy, he was terrified of dogs. His fear was not caused by a bite or an attack, which can be the source of this fear. The best we can suppose is that it came from a surprise visit from a Saint Bernard when Randy was with Ross, Devin, and the boys' great-grandpa Ed. They were in the pasture of the family farm when the neighbors' big dog meandered over for a visit. From this one seemingly insignificant event emerged an acute fear. For years, this fear affected the way Randy lived and thus the way we lived as a family. He did not like to walk to the school-bus stop, as he feared the possibility of meeting up with a loose dog. Dogs running at large always seemed to be drawn to him. He did not like to sleep overnight at friends' houses, because many of them had dogs. He loved to play T-ball and baseball at the park, but he hated to watch games from the crowd. Why? Several fans brought their dogs to the games. Even on leashes, dogs induced fear in Randy. Many thought that the immersion method would eliminate his fear. Forcing a feared animal into the face of a fearful, panicked child was not the answer, however. Our pediatrician agreed. We avoided situations where a dog might be forced upon Randy. When attempting to avoid dogs, one notices how many dogs and dog lovers there are.

Time was the answer. In time, Randy outgrew that horrific fear, but as it left him, seeds of fear were germinating in his sister. Mariah's fear of dogs was more intense than Randy's fear. Her fear was deep and included cats. It dissipated after several years, and it was then that we purchased the family beagle. A story with a *happy* ending!

Through these experiences with Randy and Mariah, fear had a face. We knew the trigger (dogs), and we knew the reactions all too well. Sheer panic was the look on their faces when they would see a dog, and the fight-or-flight reactions were prominent. For me as a parent, their fear was my fear. I could remove them from the situation and provide comfort, but I also felt helpless. I could not remove fear from them, and I learned that with time and maturity their fear would vanish. Occasionally we encounter another child with an intense fear of dogs, and our hearts go out to them in ways that can only be known by experience.

Throughout our marriage, Ross feared the return of his cancer. Sometimes a physical trigger such as an illness, a lump, or a bump would induce this fear. Sometimes the trigger would be mental. He would go along being healthy, and then he would start having that too-good-to-be-true feeling, and fear would return. His fear caused anxiety. His fear caused depression. For Ross, the return of cancer was linked to failure. Humans fear failure.

Since I was Ross's wife, his fear became my fear. I could intervene and provide comfort, but I also felt helpless. Medication could manage his anxiety and depression but could not remove his fear from him. I learned that with time, this fear would not vanish. His fear had a face that was only seen by the smallest circle of people surrounding him. I lived the closest to him and his fear, and yet, I cannot know how he felt. Through the practical knowledge that I gained from his experience, I came to understand that the fear of cancer's return is real and can only be fully understood by those who have had cancer. This fear that Ross lived and coped with became reality. In all the years I thought his fear was unjustified, in the end, perhaps, it was.

• • •

On July 4, 2010, I composed the following essay about fear, responding to the frequently asked question "How is Lynn?"

*In the Bible, angels are overwhelming creatures who carry news
that is incomprehensible and larger than life. Quite obviously,
the angels know they're scary because each message begins with
"Fear not!" Fear is a natural response for humans. In frightful situations, we need a voice (whether it be angels, other humans, ourselves, or a higher power) telling us not to fear. Fear could easily
consume us if there was nothing to counterbalance it. Think of all
life's experiences, good and bad, that can cause great fear.*

*In these months, I've had many reasons to be fearful.
Without the voices that surround me and that are a part of me,
fear would have consumed me by now. My chorus of voices has
given me determination and graced me with necessities to deal
with this heartbreaking and seemingly impossible situation.
Each person who is part of this story is included in that chorus;
Ross and I feel surrounded by a host of people—from family, to
friends, to strangers and from amateurs, to students, to experts.
In the grand scheme, everyone has a role. We are all part of
one another's lives. I've thought a lot about what we call God's
plan, and I often wonder what that is. Is it all predetermined or
does God travel with us day by day as the plan unfolds? Is God's
plan about what happens or more about response? Is God's plan
about loving and caring for one another with minds and hands
that are Christlike? If so, I feel a plan being fulfilled.*

*One night, I was listening to the sounds of Rochester in the
dark from my open hotel-room window. I heard noise—traf-
fic, sirens (remembering Ross's many ambulance rides), and
human voices. The hotel shuttle service was closing down. I had
requested my wake-up call. We'd made it through another day.*

Then I had a realization. It's not about what I'm hearing. It's about what I'm feeling. I am feeling people taking care of one another—all day, every day. The feeling is real in Rochester and at home too. Love and care are around us, close by, and spanning the miles. Our family knows it. Everyone in our circle is very dear and part of something much bigger—the kingdom that is greater than anything.

How is Lynn? I'm tired, but it's a tired that goes beyond sleep. I sleep and I eat because I know I have to. I'm learning a lot because I've had to. I'm not angry. I have a wide circle of friends and family at home, which I value deeply. I also have an ever-growing circle of friends in Rochester. I am in great care. I feel safe. I've developed a deep sense of trust. When fear begins to overwhelm me, I am able, thank God, to hear the voices that say, "Fear not!" And the journey...millimeter by millimeter... continues.

• • •

Ross did not have the fear of surgery that many of us would have. He had had dozens of surgical experiences. Anesthesia didn't scare him. He had had anesthesia so many times that his reactions were very predictable and manageable. Ross did not like surgery. For Ross, the choice, or the necessity, to have surgery meant there was hope that life could be better for him. He lived with a hope that *his* normal would someday be closer to the normal he observed in the healthy folks around him—those who were seemingly not limited or restricted.

In a conversation Ross had with the surgeon prior to his first intestinal surgery at Mayo, the surgeon sat at his bedside and was ready to talk about fear. I remember the look on the doctor's face when he posed the question to Ross, asking if he was afraid. Ross answered,

"Nope." The surgical conversation ended, and the two men continued talking—about athletic shoes!

Ross was fortunate to have reached a very high level of trust in
many doctors. The doctors, and their teams, were those earth angels
that carried *fear not* messages. Each one was confident and realistic.
Throughout this journey, we developed a strong reverence for realistic optimism and an even stronger reverence for life in general.

In July of 2010 the procedures and plans that needed to be in
place for Ross to return home from Rochester Methodist Hospital
were extensive: arranging for ultrasounds; transferring prescriptions;
setting up a home-care nurse and physical therapist; ordering his
TPN, PICC-line supplies, Hickman-catheter supplies, g-tube supplies,
and PleurX supplies. The hospital bed, wheelchair, walker, suction
machine, commode, and oxygen were being delivered to our house.
His pain was controlled, with the price of sleepiness and fuzzy thinking. Nausea, vomiting, and unease were constant issues. For reasons
both mental and physical, he couldn't be alone. Plans to return to
Rochester for the second chemo treatment were also being made. It
was an exasperating time.

Fear and *Fear Not* were fighting in my head. I was afraid, as his
life was being placed in my care. Death was at the heart of my fear. I
was afraid to have him die in my care. I feared the future. People told
me I looked fearless, and I would think back to Ross's fear of cancer's
return. Deep-seated fear cannot always be seen by the untrained
eye, but fear had a face each time I walked into Ross's hospital room
and each time I looked in the mirror.

Nine months after the first surgery at Mayo, Ross was an inpatient
at UIHC. He could not physically make the trip to Rochester. Ross had
physicians who thoughtfully communicated between the two medical
facilities. On August 22, 2010, the day after his birthday, Ross called
me close to his bedside from my cot. He told me of his wishes for pall-
bearers and music at his funeral. I was stunned at the thought that

he had put into his wishes. Then he gave me permission—to find a companion. He stated he did not want me to be alone and very matter-of-factly said that I needed someone to take care of me. He told me I took care of him better than he took care of me. As he spoke, I could tell he was feeling great relief sharing his words and thoughts.

After he said these things, he restated them in the form of an order: grieve for a while, and then find a companion. Then we argued. He wanted me to promise I would do this, and I told him I could not make the promise just then. He was angry with me. I compromised by stating that in the future, I would remember his words. I watched him fade before my very eyes as he fell into a deep sleep. The conversation probably had cathartic qualities for him, and he was able to sleep with abandon. However, as he slept, his physical state changed. His body seemed to be shutting down. The nurses were troubled by his vital signs, and they could not stir him. When I told his nurse about the conversation prior to this deep sleep, she looked at me with concern in her eyes.

I felt a wave of fear and remember asking the nurse if she thought I should call our family. She said yes. It only took a couple phone calls, and his room was filled with family. The crowd spilled into the hallway. He couldn't be roused. We were all fearful, on pins and needles that this could be the end.

Hours later in that room, in that atmosphere of sadness, Ross's eyes opened. He awoke and looked around, seeing the panic, concern, and tears of our family. Everyone had assembled for an event that pointed to the end of his life. I'm positive he was overcome by something unimaginable, and I was too. Was it fear or anger? He looked at me with fiery eyes and asked me what I had done and what I had told them. I shook with fear on the inside as thoughts swirled in my head about the death experience I thought he deserved; this wasn't it. Crowds and anger weren't working for him, or for me. If I were a person who believed in destiny and fate, I would truly believe that Ross lived for nineteen more days as his punishment to me for making those phone calls. We had no more arguments, ever, following that day.

Later he talked about his impending death with a social worker and me, and the topic of fear arose. He clearly stated that his biggest fear was to leave three kids without a dad at very important times in their lives. Devin was a soon-to-be college graduate, eager to give an engagement ring to his college sweetheart. An exciting career path was ahead of him. Randy, after a tough senior year in high school, was about to start his college career. Mariah was beginning high school. Ross spoke of the many conversations he had had with Mariah about walking her down the aisle at her wedding. Many dreams like this one had been shared during his lifetime, and those dreams would never be reality. He was afraid for what his family would face without him. He worried about the things he had left undone and grieved deeply for the future he would miss. Ross was not afraid of being sick or of death, but he was afraid of letting his kids down with his absence. To him, this was failure, laced with fear. He wore his feelings on his face as he spoke. It never showed itself again, but it was in him and could not be taken away in this life.

Many times in my adulthood, the topic of fear has surfaced—not only as the result of my experiences but also in thoughts and conversations and in dreams and illusions. From a college course, I remember a fascinating discussion about fear. What I heard, and what has remained with me from that class, is that the greatest fear is death. All fear ultimately points to death, which is usually thought of as physical death. However, we are well versed in other deaths as we experience life. Death of relationships associated with stages or events, loss of employment, and other major traumas are examples of those things that can cause death-like fear and suffering.

I have repeatedly questioned the human ability to overcome the fear of death. If a person has no fear of dying, is he or she empowered with a way of life that transcends death? Can fear be acknowledged and then shed, as to free the soul? I truly believe I witnessed Ross's shedding of fear as I witnessed his dying process.

A year later, in our quotidian life, there were significant events occurring, and I realized we were living what Ross feared most. The kids were doing all the things that teenagers and young adults do—without a dad. Devin was settling into a successful career and was planning to be married. He was meeting new people and carrying out his dreams, making a home far away from our home. Randy was driving a race car, was a member of the volunteer fire department, and was settling into his college plan. Mariah was in high school; her social life was teeming with activity. She was involved in track and was driving—taking her first solo drive to the cemetery. Loving family, friends, and teachers supported each of our children.

I was a single parent, a widow. I was still referred to as young. I became acutely aware of varying ranges of emotion. Feelings of contentment, ease, and completeness could give way to their polar opposites in an instant. In a year, my world view changed a lot. I learned new ways of observing life around me, and I learned more about myself than I ever imagined I would. I was in new territory. I could feel my grief and my children's grief taking the backseat to the busyness that surrounded us. I was somewhat startled when I realized that thoughts of loss, emptiness, and reminders of our journey were no longer the forces that drove our days.

Time was moving forward. I was feeling a wake-up of emotion. This scared me, as there had been times when I was numb to emotion. I had been enveloped in times filled with so much illness, pain, and sadness. Survival mode had overtaken me, and there had not been time to deal with my emotions. I had a burning need to maintain a standard of normalcy for my children. It wasn't normal for me to be emotional. I had packed all of my tears away and took comfort in living, doing, being, and surviving with the demands that were dealt to me. I did what I had to do at the time to get by, many days wondering if I was really okay. Fear lived with me, and at the same time I was reminding others to fear not!

Devin's wedding was in June 2012, and it was a grand event. In the midst of excitement, however, I felt that familiar pang. Yes, once again I realized we were living in the future that Ross had feared, but we were moving forward as he had wished for us. In my mixed emotion was a sense of triumph. We had not only survived, but there were times when we were thriving.

Trust

O God, in mystery and silence you are present in our lives, bringing new life out of destruction, hope out of despair, growth out of difficulty. We thank you that you do not leave us alone but labor to make us whole. Help us to perceive your unseen hand in the unfolding of our lives and to attend to the gentle guidance of your Spirit, that we may know the joy you give your people. Amen.[5]

HANDS FASCINATE ME. Study your hands. Rub them together. What do you see? What do you feel? What stories do your hands tell? How does it feel to have your hand held? Think of the times you've folded your hands in prayer or held a baby in your hands. Do you use your hands to create things? How many messes have you cleaned up, or made, with your hands? There are many occasions when a handshake is appropriate.

Do your hands resemble the hands of a family member? Have your hands changed as you've aged? Do you have cold or warm hands? Does your profession rely solely on the use of your hands? Look at the imperfections on your hands. Do you have any cuts, burns, or

---

5 Ruth C. Duck, *Bread for the Journey* (New York: The Pilgrim Press, 1981), 62.

bruises? Do you have scars, or is part of your hand missing? What do the imperfections represent?

Hands are among the first things examined on an infant. What joy and relief to hear "Ten fingers and ten toes!" when a baby is born. I can't hold a newborn without wrapping his or her little hand around my index finger. It's at that point when predictions begin about the baby's gifts and the baby's life, based on those little hands. If the baby has long fingers, of course he or she will grow to be a piano player or a musician. Babies with strong grips will grow to be sports stars. Steady hands may be the hands of a future surgeon.

Among my favorite photographs are close-ups of my kids' hands at different ages.

As children grow, their hands are in constant motion—creating countless pictures for family refrigerators, learning how to throw and catch, holding books as they learn to read, placing hands on a keyboard for piano lessons, steering a bicycle, playing video games, operating a computer, climbing, building, learning to drive. We know about sticky handprints on windows, dirty hands at the supper table, and injured hands immediately made better with a kiss and a bandage.

Our hands are extensions of God's hands. We are called to be re-creators—to heal, to feed, to teach, to work, to touch. There are visible signs that our hands are extensions of God's: sewing blankets for those who are cold, collecting and distributing food for those who are hungry, pushing a wheelchair, holding an elbow, making music, hugging children, placing bandages, wiping away tears, or holding a hand. There are invisible moments too: hands in prayer, hands wrung in concern, hands trembling in shared grief.

Hands can tell many stories. Jesus's hands tell the ultimate story of our faith, and we are commissioned to be the hands of Christ. Being the hands of Christ is a lifelong learning experience and a challenge.

In *Mornings with Henri J. M. Nouwen*, the author has this to say about hands:

A hand waits for the touch of another hand. The human hand is
so mysterious. It can create and destroy, caress and strike, make
welcoming gestures and condemning signs; it can bless and curse,
heal and wound, beg and give. A hand can become a threatening
fist as well as a symbol of safety and protection. It can be most
feared and most longed for. One of the most life-giving images
is that of human hands reaching out to each other, touching
each other, interconnecting and merging into a sign of peace and
reconciliation. In contrast, one of the most despairing images is
that of a hand stretched open, waiting to be touched with care...
Every night I go to rest and look at my hands. And I have to ask
them: "Did you reach out to one of the open hands around you
and bring a little bit of peace, hope, courage, and confidence?"[6]

When I am introduced to a doctor, his or her hands make an initial
impression on me, beginning with the handshake. Trusted surgeons
and doctors have hands that display confidence, ease, coordination,
and grace. Those observations are unequivocally connected to their
personalities and abilities. As with many professions, a doctor's hands
are integral to what they do and who they are. I often told Ross's surgeons to take care of their hands. They would promise to do that. A
few days after one of Ross's surgeries, we shared some lighthearted
moments with a surgeon who had injured his hand while doing some
landscaping work at his home. Ross chuckled, feeling fortunate his
surgery was prior to the landscaping incident.

I took care of my hands. They were integral to my role.

I look at my hands and think about all the time they spent caring for Ross: the injections, the pumps, the feeding, measuring,
recording, priming, dumping, back rubbing, and wringing in worry.
The gloves, the sanitizing, and the process of everything required

---

6 Henri J. M. Nouwen, *Mornings with Henri J. M. Nouwen: Readings and Reflections*
(Ann Arbor, MI: Servant Publications, 1997), 86–87.

so many prescribed steps. Keeping an accurate inventory and ordering supplies were huge challenges. I found notes in my journal that expressed my dislike for priming pumps and my fondness for operating syringes. How odd is that? My hands were tired, but more than that, my mind, body, and spirit were tired.

I learned a lot. I had to trust myself. Because I trusted myself, Ross trusted me. He was overwhelmed by his body. I was overwhelmed by all that was expected of me. Caregiving tasks and schedules controlled me. The people closest to our situation enabled and empowered me, allowing me total immersion into the experience. These same people helped me put myself back together in the years that followed.

Often there are things in life that push us away from developing authentic trust in human beings and systems, and our mistrust is often justified. These events in my life pulled me toward gaining trust, and I discovered that the more I could trust, the closer I was to a sense of well-being.

Ross's health situation required us to place great trust in his health care teams. We always trusted the people who made decisions on his behalf, those who helped him make decisions, and those who took care of him. In addition to trusting medical personnel, we placed great trust in other people and organizations. I trusted my kids to care for themselves and make good choices while I was away. These kids included not only Devin, Randy, and Mariah but all my kids at church. I trusted grandparents, relatives, friends, the school system, and the church community to look out for them. My household and my church continued to run without my physical presence, thanks to the efforts of dedicated people. I worried, but I trusted.

Another Advent season was approaching, the season about preparing our hearts and minds, in new ways, as we approach the birth of Jesus. This is a story we Christians trust. It's a story that reveals God's love for us. I always trusted and believed in God's love and never-ending presence.

The pregnant, expectant time of Advent came and went. Christmas 2009 passed. We continued to trudge through Ross's dark days and nights of illness. Time moved on, and Ash Wednesday was upon us. I sat in the hospital at Ross's bedside; so many things were wrong. I was tired as I thought about the words *You are dust, and to dust you shall return.* I had no ashes on my forehead, but I was deeply into the journey and, at times, overcome by the intensity of scripture.

It was Ash Wednesday when the possibility of thyroid cancer threatened. It was an intensely emotional day and the beginning of a powerful season in the church year. *My* church year. I was surrounded and ministered to by folks who were of different faith traditions, each full of faith and acknowledging a higher power. *Their* church years were not always aligned with mine, but love seemed to hold it all together.

The thyroid cancer scare was just that. The biopsy was benign.

Lent is a time when we practice dying. We walk through darkness examining our lives and asking questions. It's a time to free ourselves, ridding ourselves of what holds us back from living fully. It's a time we claim our identity as people of the Christian faith.

I once heard someone refer to Lent as a terrible gift.

Terrible gifts surrounded me that year, yet I look back and am thankful.

Ross's patience and attitude were in stages of transformation. "Just tell me where I need to be and what I need to do" was his atti-tude. Over and over, doctors reminded him of how special his case was. Ross would grumble, responding that he hated being special. Doctors trusted Ross to be someone with whom they could be open and direct. It was not necessary to tiptoe around topics as they com-municated. Trust was mutual between Ross and his array of doctors and nurses. He was at the center of so much trust and in the hands of so much expertise. The hands that held and sustained us in our living at the time were also the hands that prepared us and braced us for what was ahead.

There were many frank discussions and formidable conversations. When Ross's oncologist looked us in the eyes and said, "Trust me," we could do that completely. It's a deep human relationship, perhaps the epitome of a doctor-patient relationship, when you can trust someone so fully with not only your life but with your upcoming death. Having the opportunity to talk about it is special too. We fully recognized this.

I witnessed, and was included in, conversations between Ross and his doctors that were breathtaking, in both content and delivery. Often, the exchange of words seemed touched with the divine. Excruciating news was often conveyed at a pace that allowed for compassion, pain, emotion, and uncertainty to seep in.

The oncologist said, "When you feel good, make every moment count. Spend time with your children and family. Try to create memories and relive past memories. Think about what you want to tell your children, now and in their future."

The word *terminal* was not used, but we knew it applied, with a vengeance.

• • •

Throughout Ross's journey, we repeatedly heard the words *We'll take good care of you*. We fully trusted that promise each time we heard it. It was a promise I made to Ross, for both present and future. He knew I would fulfill my promise to take care of him. He knew I would take care of myself and our children when he was gone. I heard him tell a few other folks to take care of us, indicating his fear for our future.

On nights I didn't stay in the hospital, I left with full satisfaction that Ross was in good hands. I could shut myself into my hotel room in Rochester and lock the world out for a little while. Safety, security, and freedom were there for me because I could trust.

When Ross was on his deathbed, I took a close-up picture of his left hand to preserve a memory. He pointed to the window for three days. In an unconscious state, he pointed. This was not a normal position for his hand, but it was the position it held during those days. The nurses and I would move his hand, just to see, and it would always resume the pointed position, perhaps for no reason, or perhaps for a greater reason. We will never know. Was he pointing to light? Or to a place far away? It's something to ponder.

I observed him closely and studied his hands in those days. There were poignant resemblances to his grandparents in what I saw in him and heard from him, especially then. Ross quickly became very old. I thought a lot about how fortunate we were to be touched by the lives of many grandparents and how we trusted them.

Ross loved watching kids and had a love of dogs, just as his grandparents did. He seemed elderly in his ways of patience and compassion. I suspect this was borne from serious illness. The twinkle in his blue eyes reminded me of his grandpa. I'd see the twinkle when someone special walked into his hospital room. There was a quality in his voice, along with his choice of words, which reminded me of his grandmother. All through his life, Ross impersonated Grandpa Bill and Grandma Velma with expertise. For example, Grandma Velma would go through all kinds of contortions trying to locate tissues tucked in her sleeve, waistband, or bra. Ross did a humorous impersonation of that. Grandma Velma died four months after Ross. She was ninety-nine.

Grandpa Bill was missing a finger, and Ross had fun impersonating a trembling Grandpa Bill, pointing with an index finger that wasn't there, meaning he pointed with his middle finger! Ross knew the story behind that imperfection. Supposedly a cow had eaten it. (I'm not certain this is a story to trust.) Grandpa Bill died many years before Ross. As Ross pointed his own finger on his deathbed, I noticed it was the same finger his grandfather was missing.

We have no way of knowing, but I can imagine the grand reunion and the behavior and misbehavior taking place with the three of them in the company of the saints of light.

Tables

OFTEN WE SAY, "Let's grab a bite to eat." Bites and sips. Our bodies are dependent on nourishment. Daily manna: enough to survive as we move forward day by day. The meals we eat are usually more than just a bite. Sometimes we are known for eating and overeating, even when we're not hungry. We can consume food without thinking. We are distractible. The marketing business targets us as consumers of food.

Often, we pray, "Give us this day our daily bread." Jesus said, "I am the bread of life. Whoever comes to me will never be hungry, and whoever believes in me will never be thirsty." Our souls are also dependent on nourishment for physical and spiritual well-being. Bites and sips. "Come to the table, all who are heavy laden, and I will give you rest," says the host of the mystery-filled communion meal.

Important work is done around the table. When we approach the communion feast, we bring emptiness and fullness, hunger and thirst, distraction and focus. We remember the Body that lived for us and is living with us, symbolic of the powerful presence of God among us. Communion—a bit of bread, a sip, a spoken word—is more than a bite to eat. Is this adequate in a world spinning out of control? Does this really provide us with something that draws us closer to God?

This small meal is big. We trust that the Spirit will use this sacrament in us to bring healing and hope. We bring ourselves and our stories to the communion table. The understanding of communion is in the experience. The meaning of communion may differ, and we may be empowered in new ways, each time we commune. This sacrament meets us where we are and nourishes us, and we pray it will sustain us. Symbolic of the life it represents, it feeds us in order that we may live and serve faithfully, as we realize the joy of being satisfied.

I sat at Ross's bedside on Sunday, August 1, 2010. It was a communion Sunday at home. I was missing church again, both literally and figuratively. At that time, Ross wouldn't have been physically able to eat the bread or drink from the cup. He was in a deep slumber in his bed at Rochester Methodist Hospital. The Honker wasn't across the street from this hospital. A lot had happened in a short while, and as I sat beside him, I reflected. Thoughts of Holy Communion filled not only my mind but also the pages of my journal.

How many folks could fully experience communion without the physical elements? Are the words enough for the Spirit to intercede? I found myself communing in my mind with my congregation, miles and miles away. I had instructed the pastor to eat two pieces of bread, take a big drink from the chalice, and know that I was with my church in spirit. That particular morning, I felt God's love very near, and I communed sans bread and cup, only with words.

Feel the body, feel the blood, be filled with presence and love.
For the time that has gone by, for the time that is, for the time to come.
Take it. Let it become part of you and your living.
Reconnect with life in a new way. Refreshed and ready to move ahead.
The same, yet changed.
Come, all who are heavy laden. All is prepared.

Prepared in Christ's life and work. For me. Prepared today in the grace of God. I am here.
I've been invited into a story, and a life-changing experience.
I am mindful that it's about more than today's bread and cup.
On the night of betrayal and desertion, there was Jesus in a sacred place with his disciples.
I can picture the room, smell the room, and feel the heaviness.
Jesus said, This is my body, prepared and broken for all. Eat it.
Think about me as you do, but more than that, feel it.
Let me be a part of you, because I am.

I looked around the hospital room. I visualized the room at St. John's. In my mind, I could see faces in the sanctuary. I knew the back stories of people in the pews. I felt heaviness, tiredness, and strain. I closed my eyes and saw those for whom the feast had been prepared. We all needed nourishment.

I love the aroma of the bread, and I love raising the loaf before the bread is broken. On that day, I closed my eyes, and I was there. I pressed my thumbs into the crust and wondered, *How will the bread break?* Breaking the loaf is unpredictable. Life is unpredictable. After I broke the bread in my mind, I imagined placing my hand in the pocket of my robe to touch the white handkerchief that's always there, the white handkerchief given to me by one of those faces in the congregation. I love to break the bread. Jesus did too.

I could imagine Jesus saying, "If you can't eat the bread, that's okay. Think about me. Feel me in your life. You don't need to be here, or be physically able to eat, to think and to feel. Be fed."

Then, Jesus took the cup. Blessed what was in it for what it represented, poured it, and shared it. Poured generously, passed it around, and his friends drank. The wine, his blood, the new covenant. Now a part of them.

I see the cup being poured. I see the congregation. Thirsty.

Take and drink. If you are here or not here, if you can or if you can't, it's okay. I am with you and a part of you. Together. Now. This is us.

In my mind, I was at St. John's that morning. I missed my church family more than they knew. Ross's sound sleep was a gift on that day. There was an essence of holiness in the space of Ross's hospital room. Perhaps he felt it too. It was communion from 204 miles away. Deep thought and faith fed me to move forward.

I walked into the hallway, and a conversation from the previous day continued between a cleaning lady and me. She gave me a gift of grape tomatoes and ground cherries from her garden: my feast. Amen and amen.

• • •

Ross dealt with an unpredictable digestive system, damaged by the radiation that had obliterated his childhood cancer. As he aged, the damage became more pronounced. When he would overeat, misery would follow. Holidays were rough. It was rare that we went out to eat. In 1989 when he had a colon resection, he went for ten days without eating. He was only allowed clear liquids and IV nourishment. We thought that was drastic.

In the summer of 2009, mealtimes changed. Ross had experienced months of severe digestive difficulty and endless medical testing. He was given special diets of bland, easy-to-digest food. He ate miniscule amounts. Several prescriptions and remedies attempted to aid his digestion, and many came with a high price. I prepared runny instant potatoes, cream of wheat, pudding, and broth for him while attempting to prepare normal meals for the kids and me. Food didn't stay inside Ross's system for long.

His condition worsened. Vomiting was a daily occurrence and a constant topic of our communication. How many times, where, and how much did he vomit? He had stories about roadside vomiting, convenience-store vomiting, and leaving meetings to vomit. I remember a three-month stretch when we tallied it up and found that he'd vomited over 150 times. Conversations such as this were normal.

It appeared he didn't eat nearly enough to survive, and what he did eat would eventually come back up. Life would never be the same. At the time, we had no idea how much worse his digestive distress could be or what his system could endure.

We didn't know there would be times we'd cheer when he could eat a Popsicle or sip water, when two bites of sugar-free vanilla pudding would be considered meal advancement, or when eating a bite of egg white or a bite of applesauce would be a decision for him to make. Bites and sips were his diet. His small meals were big, and thoughts about communion would enter my mind when Ross ate.

We didn't know there would be times we'd watch him eat Jell-O and then watch the Jell-O drain out the tube in his abdomen. We'd never heard the term *borborygmi* or thought about gut sounds, but we soon became listeners. We learned the warning signs of nutrition depletion and severe dehydration, and we knew what to do when those signs were present. We knew nothing about enteral or parenteral nutrition. Little did we know that a body could be nourished without anything, nothing at all, ever entering the digestive tract. This is called total parenteral nutrition (TPN), and it's fed completely into the blood. TPN was explained as being the most nutritionally balanced diet he'd had without swallowing a thing. We quickly became experts.

All of our appetites waned the longer Ross's illness went on. Our dinner table changed. Family meals as we had known them ended. The table became a place of worry and unease. My stomach would churn as I thought about how Ross's stomach was churning. I know the kids sensed all of it.

Today, I miss mealtimes the most. Family meals are rare for many, but they were common for us, and I am thankful for the vivid, wonderful mealtime memories we have. I loved to cook, especially when my entire family loved to eat.

At the table, we caught up on the day's activities and planned for the next day. Sometimes we argued, and sometimes we ate in silence. We laughed often. Frequently, in times of better health, Ross would be late to the table due to an extended conversation with a customer on his cell phone or a chat with a neighbor in our garage or yard. I would be so mad.

The table was where Ross would sometimes burst into song, silly songs he would make up as he sang. Ask my kids about "The Yellow Song" and "The Address Song," and they'll laugh. Once Ross began singing an argument Randy and Mariah were having. The argument ended when the song began.

One time Randy threw a baked potato during supper. The dent is still in the refrigerator. We now look at that dent and don't remember the angry story behind it. It makes us smile because the dent is now a sweet reminder of a family meal. The incompleteness to our former table of five is a huge loss. Ross's chair is still at the table.

• • •

In his work, Ross sold feed for livestock. We heard about rations, ingredients, and rate of gain. There were numerous reasons for tweaking diets. Show pigs required different diets than hogs raised in confinement buildings. Cows producing milk had different nutritional needs than calves. Rabbits, chicks, and dogs had special diets. Ross loved being involved in the process of perfecting the best nutrition plan for animals. It kept him very busy. He was an expert in his field, and I would think about that as his own health care team tweaked not only his diet but also the method of feeding.

Everyone who provided Ross's care was kept busy with his many pumps, tubes, bags, poles, connections, and incisions. Taking a simple walk in the hospital hallway was a major production for him. Twice a day, a nurse would untangle all of his lines. "Order from chaos" we'd call it.

Several times I thought to myself, *Ross is going to die*. I remember the pit in my stomach and the ways I had to force myself to eat. I would go to bed feeling empty and hungry. Along with our problems at hand, more sadness would creep in as I thought of all the people who go to bed hungry. The walls of my hotel room often surrounded me in an overwhelmed state.

Our family joined us on Thanksgiving in 2009. The table was set at our hotel in Rochester. Those who could eat ate carryout. Ross, who was thankful for the two-hour pass from the hospital, sucked on a sucker.

The word *home* reentered our vocabulary after Thanksgiving. With that word came words of preparation for the stressful, scary days of extensive care. It was exciting, yet terrifying, to leave the place where the answers and experts were. Our normal, which wasn't normal, was altered. Ross's endless care would now take place alongside the realities of wrestling season, basketball season, and soon-to-be Advent season. Ross's story and the cycle of the church year eerily collided many times. The Advent and Lenten journeys, especially, will never hold the power they did in the year at Mayo.

Home-going day had a painstaking schedule of final medical tests, prescription filling, supply gathering, discharge paperwork, and many good-byes. I was terrified.

In the first twenty-four hours at home, we went from being greeted to unloading and setting up our home medical center. We were fortunate to have a second kitchen in our house. In a former time, this area had served as Ross's office, but now his medical supplies took over the room. His care commenced, and before midnight I had spoken to the nurse at the infusion company, the surgeon's resident, and the doctor in the nutrition department. When they had discharged Ross from the hospital, each of these people had said, "We'll probably talk later." They were right. Questions arose as we began home care. It was reassuring that they could all be reached with a phone call. We kept the phone lines warm and the highways traveled between home and Mayo.

At this point he weighed 135 pounds. The most he had ever weighed was 175 pounds. Rate of gain was not what we were concerned about. The goal was to eliminate loss.

On our wedding anniversary, December 10, 2009, Ross and I journeyed with Randy through snow and ice for more days of appointments. We were reminded of the ice storm on our wedding night in 1983. In my journal entry that day, I reminded my readers to enjoy the following things that don't get much thought until they are absent: the ability to eat, drink, and sleep; the ability to leave home without massive amounts of planning; the ability to shower without exhaustion; and the ability to relax with a feeling that all is well.

Stitches were removed from Ross's belly on that trip. After all the snipping was done, the surgeon pointed to the center of the radiated tissue, stating, "I'm concerned about this area. If it comes apart, don't panic. Just pack it with gauze and call me." I answered with "Okay" and noted that had happened with an incision years before. The resident handed me a package of gauze, and we headed home the next morning, Ross feeling miserable and Christmas approaching.

There were some signs of healing and forward progress, even though Ross experienced every uncomfortable gut symptom possible, almost continually, and his weight crept down. His nutrition team questioned adverse reactions to the lipids and vitamins in his TPN. They questioned malabsorption, dumping syndrome, and bacterial overgrowth in his small intestine.

It wasn't easy, but Ross was able to see Randy wrestle one match. He also rode along on a quick shopping trip. Christmas shopping was accomplished in about thirty minutes that year. The day after the shopping outing, Ross woke up very sick. To make things worse, he nearly choked on vomit. I used Heimlich-maneuver skills as best I could on his compromised abdomen. Ross said weakly, "I need to be in the hospital." The thought *He's going to die* entered my mind again.

We called, we packed, and we drove in another snowstorm to Rochester. Our furnace broke that morning too. Life was so complicated, mentally and physically. Ross not being able to eat was an incredible hurdle to overcome, and one of the many questions that loomed in his mind was *Will I ever eat again?*

We were home for Christmas. A couple days prior to the holiday, I recall Randy getting the snow-removal equipment ready for another upcoming storm, Devin making a last-minute Christmas gift, Mariah holding Chassis like a baby, and Ross sitting in his recliner hooked up to his TPN. I was cooking. For that moment, I was able to say, "All is well." There weren't many of those moments.

On February 21, 2010, Ross went to church. He was able to be unhooked and have all lines clamped long enough to attend worship. He said it felt great to be out. I have many memories of Ross in a church pew, as I would watch from my place at the front of the sanctuary. There were many Sundays I would worry about him, wondering if he would make it through the service without a problem. Throughout the years, he sat in church toting different types of medical baggage. When he wore a wound vac, Mariah would sit and giggle at the fart-like noises the suction of the vac would make. Many times the kids would show their anxiety as they sat by him. One Sunday, I was called from worship when Ross was being rushed to the hospital by ambulance.

On Sunday, February 21, 2010, his attendance at church was uneventful, but it was extraordinary that he could be there.

And so it went, more tweaking, weight loss, weakness, unease, long days, scary nights, questions. We were in and out of the hospital, craving normal. It was our life.

The day following Randy's high school graduation, we were scheduled to return to Mayo for more appointments, testing, and imaging. Ross had been feeling fairly well. Prior to our departure for Rochester, Ross's fire department pager went off. It was a call to help land the Life Guard helicopter. Ross continued to be in the fire department, but was limited to running the pump and driving. It wasn't possible for him to respond to many calls, but the call on that day was one he could manage. Landing the medical helicopter takes fire trucks parking in designated spots to guide the helicopter to the landing area.

He wasn't gone long, and when he got back, he was disgusted. The cap had come off his feeding tube while he was out. (He was on enteral feeding at the time.) This happened from time to time, and it was always a mess, but we were used to it. Stomach contents and bile had soaked through everything he was wearing. He got cleaned up, and we headed to Rochester. We were on the road when he announced we needed to find a cell phone center on the way. He said he needed a new phone.

"You sound like Mariah," I said. "She always wants a new phone."

"The feeding tube incident soaked mine. It's dead," Ross said.

"Yuck."

We stopped along the way. He went in the phone center, and I went next door to find a bite to eat. I didn't hear it, but was told the conversation in the phone center went like this:

Ross said to the dealer, "My phone got wet."

As he was checking it, the dealer said, "I'm getting some strange readings. It's not indicating it's really wet, but it's dead. It won't do anything when I plug it into the charger. It's more than just the battery."

"Yep," Ross replied.

"Your contract is up in a month, meaning you don't qualify for any special plans today. You'll have to pay full price for a new phone. I'm sure you've lost all of your contacts and information, but you could try taking your old phone completely apart. Lay it on your car's dashboard to bake. Maybe you'll get it to turn back on. If you do, bring it in and we can transfer everything."

Ross responded to the dealer with *Okay*. He paid full price for a new phone.

The new phone worked, but the old phone never again did. I enjoyed my cashews, feeling fortunate to be able to snack and smiling at this odd sequence of events.

There was nothing light or humorous about the time that followed. Life contained disturbing news and images, both in the center of our small world and on its periphery. Our family table was held together by my parents, who lived at our house when we were in Rochester. Randy and Mariah were home. Devin had moved ten hours away for an internship. We faced the cancer diagnosis in Rochester, and from there we also mourned two devastating losses of life back home: a high school student and Ross's cousin, both killed in tragic accidents. Many family tables were changed, and I often wondered if things could get worse.

Ross's condition was fragile. Critical discussions took place with his surgeon and medical team, nutritional team, physical and occupational therapists, and, added to that, his oncologists. Bits and pieces, bites and sips of conversations still ring in my ears: chemo cycles, lipid shortages, baseline scans, research, toxicity, and more. We always did better when a plan was in place. However, plans never stayed in place for long. Something always changed.

I wheeled Ross around outside as much as possible. Fresh air and sunshine had medicinal-like qualities. It made him very tired, as it did me. When we were tired, we were not always cheerful. Some days I felt like throwing potatoes at a refrigerator. My eyes would well up with tears a lot, but seldom did those tears run down my face. That scared me. Who was I becoming?

· · ·

Our hometown community of Clarence gave us the gift of a benefit to help pay expenses. It was hard to be receivers. Courage and grace met vulnerability, and we allowed ourselves to say yes to a generous offer. It was a community at its finest, and I think about the tables that folks sat around as the event was planned—at the fire station, at church, in homes, at the restaurant. I remember looking around at all the tables that were set up at our park on that day and the ways the tables were being used. Tables held items for the auction. People sat at tables to eat, drink, and socialize. Tables were everywhere. We considered it miraculous that Ross was able to be there that day. There are stories galore about the event, and there was a palpable energy, almost as if the community was taking Ross's pain away in the time he was there. He loved every minute. We have a video. I'll watch it someday.

Following the benefit, his second chemo treatment was scheduled at Mayo. Prior to the trip to Rochester, things once again turned for the worse. We made it to Mayo with the help of both of our fathers. There were so many questions about what was happening in Ross's body, and with that came great risks to starting more chemo. Ross made the decision to start the treatment, and surprisingly, chemo went well when nothing else was going well.

On the evening of July 29, 2010, with Ross in his wheelchair hooked to three different bags, I walked him around a park in Rochester. I have vivid memories of that beautiful summer evening. We watched some college students play Ultimate Frisbee. I remember thinking of those moments as being like a vacation, just as the benefit had been—bits of time to savor.

It wasn't long before he was once again turning even sicker.

Come, all who are heavy-laden...

A couple weeks later, the tired journalist in me wrote this entry:

August 9, 2010

> *Measures for comfort are still being worked out. Feeding is today's issue. They are trying tube feeding again, as there seems to be some opening in Ross's digestive system that will allow formula to pass. At Station 44, Ross continues to keep everyone on their toes. At least he was still in the hospital when his residuals got too high. (That's enteral-nutrition language.) The scene was not desirable. It is so hard for me to capture all of this in words. I continue to be in awe of the human digestive system. Fortunately, most of the population can eat and digest food without giving it thought. As I watch people, many are eating, drinking, and laughing. I think, All of their tracts are working and they aren't thinking about it at all.*

A few weeks later, the topic of food crept into my words as I crafted some life analogies from his UIHC hospital room.

> *You're either a cantaloupe person or a watermelon person. I'm a watermelon person. Ross had two bites of watermelon yesterday. This was his feast at the bedside table. A person never knows if melon is good until it's tasted. The best-looking watermelon at the store can be the most beautiful green color and thump just right on the outside but taste terrible. Sometimes I think a bad melon tastes like pumpkin or rotten tomatoes. The melon that's dirty, yellowed, and the last one in the bottom of the huge cardboard box in the produce aisle can sometimes be the tastiest one! Sometimes the bright red has no taste, and sometimes the palest is sweetest. You just don't know. Watermelons aren't*

always easy to judge from appearances. I've heard the same thing said about people. Ross's two bites of watermelon were good yesterday.

On August 21, 2010, Ross's forty-ninth birthday, UIHC provided cake. The nurse brought it in and set it on the morning newspaper on his bedside table. There was singing involved. The small cake, which Ross couldn't eat, was in a small foil pan. I took several pictures that day, and one of them happened to be of the cake on the newspaper. At the time I thought, *This is silly.* But, taking silly pictures occurs at events such as birthday parties.

I've looked at that picture often, and I no longer think it's silly. There's a story of Ross's birthday party in that picture: the bedside table, holding the newspaper with the date visible, and the simple little cake. There were parts of that day when he was happy and relished attention. He knew it was his table, his party, his birthday. The end of his life. He knew.

August 21, 2010

On this day in 1961, Ross William Butterbrodt entered the world weighing 10 pounds, 11 ounces. A big bundle of joy! Since that day, Ross has touched and influenced lives of many, many people. He's spending his birthday at UIHC, thankful for forty-nine years.

When I arose from my hospital chair, I told Ross, "Happy Birthday." He said, "Thank you. Your hair looks great." His comment about my hair was not genuine, but the thank-you was. His mom is spending the morning with him, and I came home to work on my bad hair, among other things.

Here's what's been going on: Ross was expedited through the ER on Thursday night. The twelve hours that followed were among the worst ever. We are now blessed to be on holy ground, in a private room, at UIHC. Ross has another serious infection. He's also being treated for pneumonia. He spent the last couple days with a 103-degree fever. It broke during the night, and his temperature has been very low since. That's a concern too. He's comfortable, being very patient, passive, soft-spoken, and friendly. He loves to sleep. Happy birthday, Ross!

On September 1, 2010, Ross ate his last meal for pleasure. I'm not sure if the pleasure balanced the misery that followed. In a former time, I would have begged him not to eat, and the result of the mealtime experience would have prompted an *I-told-you-so* lecture from me. This wasn't the case that day. For his last meal, at noon, Ross ate pork served on a bed of white rice. He insisted he needed the experience of chewing, tasting, and swallowing. He knew he shouldn't eat anything by mouth, but as he ate, he also said it tasted good. Then misery set in.

The nurse and I spent the afternoon hours doing nearly unimaginable things, trying to decompress his stomach. His meal was obviously stuck and needed to be evacuated. We suctioned rice and meat from his g-tube, very slowly, sometimes one grain of rice at a time. We positioned and repositioned him. He moaned in pain. We cried. Finally, with all the energy he could muster, he vomited himself empty. Then he was moved to his room in the palliative care wing of the hospital. The remainder of the night was spent trying to stay ahead of his nausea. By morning, this was accomplished. Most medications were given through his PICC line. He was still swallowing a few pills, but drinking sips of liquid caused him to cough. He got hiccups following drinks. Doctors continued to find medical remedies to ease his discomfort.

I learned a lot about survival in those days. I learned a lot about diverse gifts that are given and received around tables. Eating and communing would never be the same for me; however, years later I can startle myself with a flashback when I find myself eating, drinking, grazing, or snacking with reckless abandon. Sometimes I feel guilty.

I remember words and fragments, and I remember the words from communion, *Let me be a part of you, because I am.*

This is all part of me.

Doors and Passages

IN OUR HOME, there is a framed picture of the revolving door at Saint Mary's Hospital in Rochester, Minnesota. Why? The reason is twofold. (I'll get to the second part of the reason at the end of this chapter.) First, the picture reminds us of the experience that produced the most intense laughter ever from all three of my children at once. When the door is mentioned, laughter is still produced, and it's my guess that will always be the case.

The revolving doors at Mayo meet all standards for accessibility. They're big, and they move at a speed that perfectly accommodates a wheelchair or walker. However, they don't move *too* slowly. If you walk *too* slowly, a friendly and professional female voice says, "Please move forward."

She is in all the revolving doors. We would often joke about her important job, wondering where her control station was located on the Mayo campus. We deemed her very necessary, carrying a responsibility for people entering and exiting buildings.

One evening, the kids were on their own getting from the hotel to Saint Mary's Hospital. They hopped off the hotel shuttle and entered the hospital. It was their first experience with the revolving door and the woman. Evidently, they did not move at the appropriate speed as they walked in the door, and the woman had to say, "Please move forward." Doing so, Randy moved forward right into the glass, creating a sound and a sight big enough to not only embarrass him and his siblings but to send them into hysterics. They burst into Ross's room, filled with laughter that was contagious. We all laughed very hard before Ross and I even heard the story.

We became friends with the voice in the revolving doors. The conversations we had about her were comical and provided laughter that was like medicine. We joked about the possibility that we'd lost our minds.

We would also question our sanity with a people-watching game we played. When we saw a person who looked like someone back home, we'd say his or her name and then point out the differences we noticed. Sometimes at the end of a day, we'd list all of the people from home we had seen—another example of a time we'd laugh on the outside but cry on the inside. We craved some lightness, so we concocted bright spots in our dark days.

• • •

I like to think about the doors in daily routines, the ordinary doors and the extraordinary doors. There are home doors, work doors, church doors, school doors, store doors, and car doors. Doors lead to favorite and dreaded places, opening and closing. Many doors exist only in our minds. When we walk through a door, we came from somewhere, and we're going somewhere.

There's a chapel at Saint Mary's Hospital that is awe-inspiring. A simple passageway allows entrance to that grand, ornate, and most holy of spaces. The first time we walked into the chapel, I was pushing Ross in a wheelchair. It hadn't been a good day. We were out of his hospital room, craving some brightness. I can still visualize our expressions when we saw the chapel for the first time. It was very much like an initial view of mountains or ocean.

After that, I regarded myself a chapel tour guide for our visitors. Ross was not always feeling well enough to make the chapel trip with us, so while he would rest in his hospital room, I would walk folks to the chapel. I loved seeing the faces of those who experienced the magnificence of the chapel for the first time. Walking through the chapel door filled me with a sense of the extraordinary.

The revolving door at Saint Mary's became an ordinary door for me. It was familiar and part of my everyday routine. After I entered the revolving door, my path was always the same. I'd turn down a short hallway, round another corner, and then enter the longest hallway I've ever known. I walked it, and prayed it, many times each day. That doorway and hallway were passages. I took pictures to preserve the memory.

Questioning always took place in my mind as I walked, as I wondered what I would find when I arrived at Ross's bedside. Just like the chapel, the hallway was a sanctuary for me as I walked, thought, and prayed. It represented dread and hope. It was part of a system and a community; it was a place that I will treasure forever: a simple, long, and deep hallway, sometimes noisy and bustling, sometimes quiet, eerie, and dim. A straight labyrinth, it was a path that represented a life-changing time.

There are many paths we take each and every day: the doors, the hallways, the streets. What fills these paths? Dread, fear, and loneliness? Or fullness, wholeness, and hope?

I was filled with images of doors, as there were many of those figurative doors opening and closing in life around me.

During the time Ross was at Saint Mary's, our house had four red exterior doors. The two in front were rarely used. Of the two in back, one was used all the time, and the other door went nowhere at the time. (Yes, you read correctly. It went nowhere.) The door that went nowhere was on the second floor of our split-level home, in the kitchen. The previous homeowner had plans for that door to lead to a deck, but the deck wasn't built. We opted not to build a deck and planned to eventually make that door disappear. If nothing else, the door that went nowhere was a conversation piece.

I mentioned the doors being red. There was a time I had a plan to change the color scheme from red to forest-moss green. This seemed like a minor spruce-up as we anticipated and prepared for the May 2010 confirmation and graduation celebrations at our house. Plans were altered that spring, and the color-changing spruce-up didn't happen.

During a sleepless night, I was thinking about the doors that open in May for young people. As confirmands affirm their baptisms and become adult members of the church, they stand at a threshold of their journeys of faith.

Doors that have become familiar will become doors of the past for those graduating from high school. New doors—of all different colors and sizes—are in the future. What really matters is not necessarily how the doors look but how they function and what they represent. There are many analogies that can be made between doors and life.

There are doors that go nowhere. I had one in my kitchen that could be seen and touched. It was real, and we lived with it. I was certain that door would disappear and the other doors would be green someday. I would control that.

We all know about those figurative doors in our lives that go nowhere: those places of uncertainty, disappointment, loneliness, doubt, anxiety, fatigue, illness, grief, sadness, and more. Those doors are real, and we lived with them too, when we seemed out of control.

May 2010 was a month we will never forget. It was a threshold, gift-like month. Ross's health was not good, but we were allowed to breathe a bit easier for the month of May as we celebrated milestone events in our family. We entered May from previous months of great difficulty. What we didn't know then was that the door to June would lead to an even more arduous journey.

As for my house doors, four new doors were installed, and the new paint color wasn't green. It was a shade of red called cherry bark. Mariah wanted to keep the doors red and familiar. I agreed. The door that went nowhere didn't disappear. It was replaced, painted red, and goes somewhere. A deck was built. The passage of time alters plans.

• • •

To conclude my thoughts about the revolving door at Saint Mary's, when the kids and I left the hospital the night of the laughing incident, we rounded the corner and saw the revolving door, causing them to once again burst into laughter. They relived that hilarious moment, and I had tears of laughter rolling down my cheeks. The security guard at the entrance watched us, smiling. When we got through the door, the guard, with dry humor, looked at Randy and said, "Break your nose?" That did it! We laughed our way back to the hotel and continue to laugh about the incident to this day.

Do you remember when I said the reason for the framed picture was twofold? The second reason serves as another reminder: you cannot enter those doors and not be changed.

Edges

I DON'T LIKE edges. High, unguarded edges leave me trembling and weak in the knees. I keep my distance. As a mom, I have a self-imposed duty to keep my kids away from edges. Or, I should say, *try* to keep my kids away. They know how I feel. They don't feel the same way, and there is frequent bantering between us on this topic. They razz me about our family vacation to the Black Hills, when quite often I found myself pulling them and others away from high edges that didn't have a protective device or bumper to keep stumbling tourists from falling down into the wooded ravines surrounding Mount Rushmore. I've tried to gracefully accept their taunting. Mind you, it's not heights that I'm afraid of. It's the feeling of not being safe, of falling into unknown territory, alone and unprotected. I have no desire to experience free-falling. The mere idea makes me sweaty. This is fear. And at the core of fear is death.

This is about being on an edge—that edge between life and death, where we lived for quite a while. We were on a brink, a threshold, where life was on one side and death on the other. For the rest of my life, I will relive, rethink, and reprocess that time. Living on a threshold isn't easy, but it can be a sacred, holy place. It was for me. I felt safe. I felt secure. I was immersed. I was calm, cool, and collected but also out of control. Together, the kids and I decided what protection they needed on this edge, when they needed to step back and return to the life-side. This was a once-in-a-lifetime and once-in-a-death-time experience. Death wasn't feared. I wasn't alone. But there was a lot of unknown territory that I would fall into. For forever.

At death's periphery, I actively observed. My observations are what prepared me, educated me, and secured me. I was on the threshold of life—a changed life. Ross was on the threshold of life and death. I observed his edge behavior and marveled daily at what was happening before my eyes.

As an elementary student, I remember learning about snakes shedding their skin. I was fascinated as I heard the science teacher describe this process in detail and as I witnessed the molting process of the small snake that lived in the classroom. That was big stuff back in the early 1970s, a living science experiment in an elementary classroom in Clarence, Iowa. The eyes of the class were opened, and following that lesson, we would look for snake skins on the playground, in our house yards and barnyards, and on our walks to and from school. Several snakeskins found their way to school for show-and-tell. This was science, and this was real life.

Snakes shed their skin. Caterpillars transform. They slough, or cast off, what is no longer needed, and a new phase begins. Trees shed their leaves. The leaves drop and scatter, exposing the tree to its next cycle of existence. We learn about these things early in life. We don't have difficulty with shedding imagery when we talk about molting skin or falling leaves.

My kids would walk in the house after a school day and they would shed. They'd arrive home, and possessions from the day seemed to slough from them—the shoes, the coats, the hats, the mittens, the book bags, the socks, the pocket contents, the sweatshirts. Usually the path of items could be followed to the refrigerator. My boys were good at shedding, but my daughter out shed them. I could follow Mariah's path and have an indication of her day by the order and contents of what she shed. There seemed to be a freeing quality to the shedding that took place after school, much like the freeing quality of babies and infants when they remove clothes from themselves and each other. Before Ross and I had children of our own, we lived by a family with twin girls who spent most of their summer days without clothes. They helped one another get naked. They played with reckless abandon, unconstrained and free of what was in their way.

Throughout life, we shed things like pounds, tears, debt, and relationships. This metaphysical shedding represents a freeing of accumulation. We are made lighter in literal and figurative ways when we shed. This metamorphosis can be liberating and life changing.

So it was as Ross prepared himself and as we prepared ourselves for what we faced.

I had the desire to comprehend everything about his condition. We reached a point when I wasn't sure that my understanding mattered, but it felt like information was my protection. Ross was so sick, and there were times I wondered if he had a true comprehension of all that was wrong in his body. I was sure he didn't try to comprehend, and his understanding probably didn't matter.

As I've mentioned before, when Ross first got the diagnosis, he stated, "My cancer came back. This is not going to end well." In those long days following the diagnosis, perhaps he understood more than I gave him credit for. Those words were possibly the beginning of his shedding process.

The planner in me wanted to know when he would die, but I came to realize the power and purpose in mystery. I needed to give myself permission to live in, and trust, the present, with some acceptance of the unknown. I balanced on that threshold. Ross didn't want to die but knew he was dying. He was not in a hurry. The goal throughout August 2010 was to have good days, one at a time. Each of us experienced profound sadness during this time. We were together as a family as much as possible.

Breathing the air of home was always refreshing after hospitalization. Home felt quiet, safe, secure, restful, and peaceful. Yet there was great safety, security, and protection in the hospital setting. There were times we preferred one setting to the other, and other times we didn't know where we wanted to be.

We were home for a short stretch of time in July 2010. There was some predictability to the complicated daily schedule. Ross had rather regular periods of sleepiness, alertness, and fever. Difficulty breathing produced some scary situations, especially at night. I came to dislike nighttime. Nights were not only dark but also scary, restless, and uncertain. I would enter nighttime with dread, wondering how we'd make it through and if Ross would live until morning. The sun always rose the next day, and I remember uttering my prayer, "Thank you, God," each morning.

A year earlier, I had disliked mornings. Mornings had been terrible. He didn't feel well, and each morning was the brink of another ill day. I worried about making it through each day. By night, he was literally empty from throwing up and was so tired, but he usually felt better. I had liked night back then, because it meant we had made it through another day. "Thank you, God" was my bedtime prayer then.

In late summer 2010, losing my mind was not an option, so I lost my keys instead. I remember being amazed that only my keys had been lost in all the shuffling. There were opportunities to lose so much more.

August 18, 2010, was a memorable day. Ross had a constant fever, was very sleepy, and was on a new antinausea medication that had been added to the schedule. He was very quiet but wanted to go outside late in the afternoon. We did. We even managed a walk around the park. Ross enjoyed the wheelchair ride. Randy, Mariah, Chassis, and I enjoyed the walk.

That evening, we had some special visitors. They brought groceries to us. Later that evening, Randy and Mariah went to a friend's farm to watch baby pigs come into the world. Mariah was in awe and took forty-one pictures for Ross to see. Forty-one. Oh, the excitement of Iowa! Mariah stated that seeing pigs being born changed her life.

A friend who saw us walking in the park wrote a message telling us we had been a beautiful sight. It felt beautiful. It was more than a walk, and I can replay the special visit in my mind. That night was Ross's last night at home, ever. The next day he entered UIHC.

There was a commission we often used at church, containing a biblical line about running the race with patience. That's what we did. I began sleeping in a cot next to Ross in his hospital room. He didn't want to be alone, but he also couldn't handle much company. Sometimes I didn't know what to say to him, so I'd simply remind him that I was right there with him, just as I had done so often at home. That seemed to calm him, and he would reply, "Okay." He said *okay* a lot and I noted it several times in my journal. It was code for *I'm still alive, I hear you, I appreciate your presence, and thank you.* It was easier for him to say *okay* than to say more words.

On August 31, 2010, I wrote the following journal entry, from our edge:

The UIHC doctor who knows Ross best is back from vacation. This doctor can see this situation as a whole. He has been Ross's doctor for many years. His wisdom and guidance will lead this journey onward. He helped Ross with decisions today. More pain medication has been scheduled. No pain today. Nausea is con-trolled by three medications. Ross hasn't had tube feedings or IV hydration for forty-eight hours. Those tubes are unhooked, and he's not missing the tubing or what ran through it. He has taken a few bites of food—for pleasure. He sips on clear liquids. He is not hungry. No nausea. After six years, blood thinners have been eliminated. His lifetime prescription of Coumadin ended. Ross said, "No more." He is in control, and those words repre-sented a turning point. Aside from monitoring his infection, they have eliminated daily blood draws. All the medications he's on, and there are many, are for his comfort. Care-wise, it has been a much simpler day. Ross felt better today too. He had visitors, which he appreciates, but visits really wear him out. Per the doctor's advice, nurses are cracking down on the fifteen-minute, two-people-at-a-time limit. When you observe Ross for an entire day, it's easy to understand why he can't handle more. His face for visitors is so different from the face I see. Palliative care has begun. When a room opens up in the palliative care unit of the hospital, Ross will be moved there from the medical floor where he has lived for a couple weeks. The atmosphere there will be different.

Here are a few observations: I'm not a fan of clutter. Clutter has never bothered Ross. He doesn't even notice clutter. If you've ever seen his office, ridden in his vehicle, or been in his garage, then you know what I mean! I like quiet. Ross doesn't notice noise. I can smell anything from miles away. Ross can't. It drives him crazy when I smell natural gas, something hot, or smoke. He couldn't even smell dirty diapers, so it never occurred to him to change them when we had babies!

In the past couple days, this has all changed. Ross has become sensitive to smell, noise, and clutter. The hospital got new pillows. He can't stand the smell. He also questioned the smell of his deodorant. I have to declutter his bedside table every night, and he likes it best when the excess baggage from the room is out of his sight. The hallway noise really bothers him. I think this new noise aversion is why he's having difficulty with conversation with more than two people in the room.

The next day, he settled into a room in the palliative care unit. That day, a former coworker and friend wrote a private message online. It said

Ross, few leave footprints that are hard to follow, but you have! You will remain part of every life you've touched. Few people can say that in their lifetime. The memories that have been made will always be in our hearts. May we all continue to live by the example you've shown. For a

quiet man, what can I say but "Wow!" Sending hugs that encircle you with hope, warmth, strength, and never-ending love.

This was the last message I read to Ross. He didn't want to hear more. On the edge where he teetered, he was shedding. After hearing this last message, Ross said, "That was good." He shut himself off from taking in any more words or acts from friends. He was full. He held all of his friends close to his heart, but he also knew he had to let those earthly relationships go. He was releasing himself.

With this shift, I wrote with a different, perhaps more reflective, style in the online journal. The responses changed too. The words were therapy for those who were grieving and who would grieve for a long time to come, myself included. There was great beauty and depth to the words that were shared on the journey while it was being lived. Those same words have new meaning for me each time I reread them.

September 2, 2010

Ross was quieter, weaker, and very drawn today. He slept most of the day, except when I strolled him outside in his wheelchair. There have been promises made to him. Nausea will be controlled, and he will have no more physical pain. Each day, we will inventory and make sure these promises have been kept, make sure each of our kids is okay, and make sure that I'm okay. Today, everyone is okay—sad, but okay. For Ross, who is the sickest of the sick, the worst days have passed. I can go back into the archives of my notebooks and find many days that have been worse than these, with excruciating pain, nausea, and unease.

Here is a bit of preaching for you to ponder: My very personal definition of hell is the absence of God. I do not believe that God is ever absent. It's human nature to doubt. So therefore, we are not going through hell, nor have we ever. God has been closely present in all we have endured, and God is very present as we walk through the valley of the shadow of death.

The responses to this post were powerful. Reality was oozing in, and those who loved Ross dearly were with him in spirit on the threshold. They were walking with us through the valley, holding us in love and prayers, comforting us with deep, thoughtful, theological words. One friend wrote about great lessons Ross has taught: love your family unconditionally, fight the good fight faithfully, adore a puppy even if she's a bit feisty, make memories with your kids doing the things you love to do together, support your friends no matter what they're going through, let your family and friends embrace you and journey with you even in the toughest of times, and water the grass. Another wrote, *You have a quiet strength that is just present. No words need to be said.* One friend painted a picture in words of angels assembling in heaven. I remember thinking, *Angels have assembled on earth too.*

Often the promise of God's presence was felt in the people who surrounded us. At times when my faith felt tested, I was reminded of how this very faith provides hope in and for something so great that death cannot impede it.

September 3, 2010, was Ross's Grandma Velma's ninety-ninth birthday. I shared this tribute:

There are many ways that Grams and Ross are alike. They are both ornery (especially with one another), love to talk, and have some twist to their sense of humor. They've lived well and love to laugh. Family means the most to them. Coincidentally, both are parents to two boys and one girl. They share the qualities of patience, endurance, and trust in others. Both have great faith. Both have lived well and earned the right to take off their clothes, sit by the window, and sing. (Most of you will not understand this.) Tonight, Ross looks like he's ninety-nine years old. Happy birthday, Grams!

Two days later, it seemed as though Ross was slipping away. I whispered to him, "We're all okay. It's okay for you to die." He whispered back, "I know, but I'm not in a hurry." And he wasn't. He continued a schedule that repeatedly went from uneasy to nauseous to extremely tired. He kept everyone busy as they worked, keeping the promises made to him. There were no pain issues, but he went through all classes of antinausea medication. Every time I would settle down, he would need something. It was just like home!

His extreme behavior and demands continued, as I wrote in these journal entries:

We were going for a walk with him in the wheelchair, when suddenly he wanted to shower. He hasn't been up to shower for a week, but we got it accomplished. He's eating Popsicle after Popsicle. They go down his throat and out his g-tube, but he's enjoying each one to the max. He said, "See, I told you I'd eat again." Sometimes he is right on with what he's talking about, but sometimes he's living back in time. He is showing me that orneriness that he and Grandma Velma share! He's also been talking nonstop.

He tries to get up, just to yank my chain. Randy, it's like you said. It's like when I'd walk into the garage and Dad would pick up something heavy, just to see my reaction. (Ross wasn't supposed to lift over ten pounds and usually obeyed this restriction; however, he liked to rouse me by threatening to lift.)

Ross's nurse is helping me, and, working together, Ross is getting everything he wants, including the toothpick to get the chicken (?!) out of his teeth. There isn't any chicken there. We chose to laugh about this.

Yes, it's been interesting. There's an exhausting sweetness to it, because I know what will follow this surge of energy. He's not in any hurry but knows it's all okay.
September 6, 2010, 2:00 p.m.
Ross is still "busy" and entertained by things that I'm not seeing. We'll say he's happy. The hospital gowns were the same at UIHC and Mayo. They're the same blue color with a design of

random patterns of clustered dots. Today Ross is studying those dots intently, fascinated by them. To him, these dots are bugs, and they are populating. I think back to the garden at Rochester Methodist Hospital. Six weeks ago, we watched as a butterfly landed on this same blue-patterned gown.

He has been extremely *polite and thankful to everyone, in both of his worlds.*

During the night, I was hearing the rattle from his chest. I got up to move closer for a listen, wondering if I'd wake him and wondering what nice, angelic thing he would say to me if he woke. He did wake, and upon opening his eyes, he said to me, "You have horns."

"Growing out of my head?" I questioned.

"It's your hair," Ross said. "It looks bad, but I wouldn't worry about it."

My bad hair strikes again!

He pulled a deep, deep slumber this morning. The question loomed: Will this be it? *Then he somehow reminded himself that he wasn't in any hurry, because he woke up and needed a Popsicle and a Sprite. He didn't eat, just stirred the Popsicle in the Sprite. Now* Dirty Jobs *is on TV, and he's laughing at the pig in his bed and Mr. Squirrel that keeps hiding in the room! These past two days have contained pure joy! The kids are bringing more clothes to the hospital for me. I'm out of clean clothes and tired of rewearing socks. Working on Labor Day.*
10:00 p.m.

The room is quiet and darkened again. I'm not a fan of night. Ross is quieting down, but his mind is still going to places I don't understand. There are no words to fully explain his energy surge. He has been comfortable, but he's very confused. These past two days have been the strangest ever, and he should be so tired. We decided he'd break a mind machine if we hooked him up. I have wondered many times if this is really happening. Mariah told him

today that he still gives strong hugs. Ross told her that's so she
always remembers him.
Back to the dark room.

The last time our kids and Ross saw one another was during Labor Day weekend. All three visited the hospital on Sunday afternoon. Then Devin returned to college. On Monday, Randy and Mariah brought Ross a slush drink when they came, accompanied by my parents. Ross's fascination was in stirring, not sipping. We will never know why. After the visit, final hugs and good-byes happened. The kids started walking out of the room. He had been busy with the straw in his drink and had taken a piece of the straw's wrapper to make a spit wad. He said, "Ri" (this is how we shorten Mariah's name), calling the kids back. They turned around, and he attempted to shoot the spit wad at them! This is an odd and extremely humorous final memory for Randy and Mariah.

Another step in Ross's dying experience was complete.

We made a choice that Ross would not die at home. Ross would have loved to see home again, but he honored the wishes of Devin, Randy, and Mariah. The kids did not wish to be present at the end. They did not want that memory, and I didn't want them to live with an uncomfortable memory. Thoughtful, prayerful consideration was given to where his death would take place. It was a decision we wrestled with, and it was the right one for us. Ross was comfortable in the room where his life ended. Our home contains vivid memories of him being very sick, but it does not contain a memory of the place he died. Our home holds life memories. Some of the best doctors in the world helped us to make this decision. I'm thankful.

Decisions were heavy weights on the edge where we lived.

September 8, 2010, 1:30 a.m.
   The will to live. There is a tangle between heaven and earth
happening in the dark, quiet, spirit-filled hospital room. All I

can really do is observe and attempt to interpret. I am filled with awe.

After about twenty hours of sound sleep, Ross awoke and waved at me. He cannot talk, but with his gestures, he communicated to go into the bathroom. It was all the nurse and I could do to get him there, but he went. Then he washed his hands. Returning to bed, he gestured for a drink and took a semiconscious slurp through the straw. Output and input. Perhaps his last physical acts?

The spirit inside him is so strong. It is a privilege to be where I am right now, alone. And it has to be this way. The nurse whispered, "Wow" when we had him settled back in his bed.

September 9, 2010

Maybe it is Ross's extremely diminished condition. Maybe it's the state I'm in. Maybe it's the phase of the moon. For whatever reason(s), Ross, the nurse, and I didn't get along. I had to growl. That helped. After the growl, the three of us did fine together all night. At 5:00 a.m., the nurse gave Ross more medication through his PICC. He mouthed a slight "thank you" and tried to shake her hand. I think he even had a smile. He looked like his Grandpa Bill. Pretty sweet. I'm still listening to the cadence of his breathing.

A lot of reflection happened in those days of palliative care as I waited.

On November 5, 2009, I had posted in the online journal as we were waiting in Rochester during the time between appointments and Ross's surgery. We had a week to wait. Dr. Seuss's book *Oh, the Places You'll Go!* includes two stanzas about The Waiting Place, for people just waiting. Everyone is just waiting. The Waiting Place is *a most useless place*, according to Dr. Seuss.[7] In 2009 I didn't agree

---

7   Dr. Seuss, *Oh, the Places You'll Go!* (New York: Random House, 1988).

with Dr. Seuss about *useless*, but I agreed that everyone is waiting for something. As I experienced a lot of waiting during the time of Ross's illnesses, there were times when I felt useless, but I've come to realize that the gift of time, of waiting, is useful.

> *September 10, 2010, 8:23 a.m.*
> *There has been time for reflecting and re-reflecting. This is all I have this morning:*
> *Dear Ross,*
> *For all those times I was ready to leave an event, and you wanted to stay and visit, but we left for me: I am thinking about those times and am kind of sorry. I'm staying for this one, as long as you do. And I know you're in no hurry.*
> *Love, Lynn*

Cancer is a big diagnosis. Death is a big concept. I don't know what it's like to be the person on the threshold, dying.

At UIHC there are four rooms devoted to palliative care in a section of the hospital referred to as the Unit. When the Unit is full, each contains a patient who is dying a unique death. Four circles of different sizes. Four sets of promises. Four death rattles. Doctors and nurses and more: professionals who live in this atmosphere day to day, year to year. It's their normal. They know the patterns death takes, and they know there are surprises. They've experienced typical and atypical behavior. This is new for me, this intimacy. I'm hypersensitive.

Decades ago, an aunt shared some words of wisdom with me: *You do what you have to at the time to get by.* Those words were especially meaningful when I had three young children and was managing a schedule that at times seemed impossible. Those words were especially meaningful in the days, months, and years of Ross's illnesses. With love and care of those around me, doing what I had to was eased. Other people took care of my house, my job, my day-to-day work and responsibilities, and my beloved children so that I could be where I needed to be at the time. I was getting by. Others gave me a gift so that my complete presence could be at Ross's bedside. There were times when it felt as though time were standing still, things would always be that way, and middle-earth would forever be normal.

When we decided that the kids would not be present for Ross's death, we also decided that I would be the only one present. Ross and I made that decision together. We were blessed with so much love and so many people in our lives. We could have instantly had a room, hallway, and lounge filled with those closest to us as we waited. But that was not the case. My memory of our last argument a few weeks earlier justified the decision. Turning our plan into reality felt like a gift I could give him. I will never know if he recognized the complete-ness of my gift, but he gave me signs along the way that pointed to his understanding.

As we inched along, we held our breath as we neared our vantage point: the edge where we lived, where time stood still, and where transformation was about to take place.

Reality

The woods are lovely, dark and deep.
But I have promises to keep,
And miles to go before I sleep,
And miles to go before I sleep.
Robert Frost, "Stopping by Woods on a Snowy Evening"

IT WAS 1982, and I was enrolled in English III at Cornell College in Mount Vernon, Iowa. In the class, Robert Frost's poetry was dissected around a heavy library table in an unadorned classroom located in an antiquated brick building. The setting breathed an ethos of higher learning. As the small class was drawn into each poem, the room overflowed with the persona of Dr. Elizabeth Isaacs. She was old, passionately intelligent, and fearfully mysterious. She displayed confidence and kindled respect on both the giving and receiving ends.

Elizabeth Isaacs was a professor who invited classes into her home, insisting that intellectual development was stimulated by experiences outside the classroom. Her quaint home was exactly as one would expect. A home of character and understated furnishings but filled with treasures that told the story of her life. A life immersed in language and poetry. We sat in nervous awe, sipping tea from bone-china cups. We were college students with undeveloped cup-and-saucer skills.

Dr. Isaacs knew Frost's poetry inside out and upside down.

As the snow in the poem swirled in the poetic woods, rumor of her intimate friendship with Robert Frost, the poet, swirled throughout the class members. The rumor was never confirmed, but it added to the aura that surrounded Elizabeth Isaacs. We knew her as a teacher, unaware of the treasure she buried deep inside her being.

Dr. Seuss was once quoted as saying, "You can get help from teachers, but you are going to have to learn a lot by yourself, sitting alone in a room."

Ross's room in the Unit was lovely, dark, and deep. It was a simple room, uncluttered in his process of shedding. I slept on a cot and lived lightly. There was my bag for clothes and toiletries and another bag with books, journals, and information. These bags were tucked away out of Ross's sight, by his request. His requests were honored. Promises were kept. The burden I carried was deep inside my being.

In those final days, Ross's possessions at the hospital, a few toiletry items, would have fit into a sandwich bag. His wedding ring was on a chain around my neck. He wore a familiar blue hospital gown, no longer hallucinating about the fabric pattern. His own orange and yellow bands never left his wrist. I would look at those bands and think, *Shit does happen*. There was not one *thing* that had meaning to him, and the process of getting there was a process to behold. Ross had turned into a very old man before my eyes. I felt like a very old woman.

His room was nestled into a quiet corner of the fourth floor of UIHC. A long, twisting-and-turning labyrinth of a hall had to be walked to reach the room. The change in atmosphere was palpable the closer you got to the Unit. The sights and sounds of care, treatment, and therapy were replaced by the quiet hush of impending death: the cadence of breath, the essence of mystery. There was an aura in the room. One nurse described it as a feeling of having to separate the air as she entered. I am still in awe about what overtook his room, where we seemed to travel for miles and miles without changing location. From the outside looking in, one could not know everything that was going on inside Ross's body or mind. It was that way from the beginning.

• • •

In the twenty-eighth chapter of Genesis, Jacob, the biblical dreamer, appears. We hear of the dream he dreamed on a big stone, in a dark and nameless place. In the dream, the ladder is firmly planted on the ground with its top touching the sky. Uncanny messengers are climbing the ladder, and holy ones are returning. And there's God, making promises and blessing Jacob's family so they can bless all families of the earth—including us. These blessings from God seem to contain both opportunity and burden. Jacob wakes with a start and claims that the Lord is where he is. There wasn't a temple or shrine there. Really, nothing seemed special about the place at all. Yet because of this dream, the place became awe-inspiring. A "noplace" was transformed into a holy place. Jacob's grogginess disappeared, and so did the ladder. Reality was altered, and life was changed because of this dream. Jacob went on his way, not feeling alone because of God's presence with him.

There is a good reminder for us in this story. Religion might make its home in a church sanctuary. A sanctuary may have homelike or refuge-like qualities. It may feel safe and definitely may feel like a place that is close to God. But Jacob reminds us that God isn't confined to a sanctuary. God is everywhere, even when the setting doesn't seem to be special or holy. Wherever we are, God is.

God was with us in all the sacred spaces of this journey. Our home, clinics, the hotel, the Honker, Saint Mary's chapel, and shuttle rides. They were all sanctuaries. There were sacred words in all communication. There was holiness in each of Ross's many hospital rooms, especially the last one.

In all its holiness, the process of Ross's death was painstaking and grueling. It was nearly unbearable to watch him as his breathing became more and more labored, his death rattle reaching its peak. There were earplugs available for me.

A magical blue gel was placed in a cup, absorbing the odor of lingering death that overtook the room. There seemed to be a solution for each issue and the collective accumulation of issues. Be mindful, I had undeveloped death skills, but the nurses and doctors with us were death experts.

The promise of comfort was kept. Ross was given morphine in short intervals. The nurses gracefully and purposefully alternated between rooms, keeping promises. Fluid was overtaking Ross's lungs as sepsis overtook his body. Intervention failed, and he died. It was Friday night, September 10, 2010, at 9:39 p.m.

Decades were erased from his appearance as complete peace swept over him. For a few moments, time stood still. The nurse was out of the room when it happened.

I hope Ross dies at night with only me there.

The dream became reality.

The world outside the hospital was busy and bustling. Down the hall and in the next room, time marched on.

That was the moment that changed life. That was the twinkle of the eye, the last trumpet, in scripture. At that moment, we lost a dad, a son, a brother, a friend, a husband, and more.

When the nurse returned, there was a shift in care. I was at the center. There was a promise to care for Ross's body while caring for my spirit. Words that surrounded me in those moments provided comfort and fed me for the immediate future I faced. I had to leave, for I had news to share.

• • •

Time after time, Ross's major surgeries were noted as difficult but went as well as could be expected. He handled anesthesia remarkably well. In fact, through the years they fine-tuned his anesthesia so precisely that I referred to it as medical art. Ross handled surgery well, but he did not heal well. Poor healing became an expectation after each surgery. Healing is hard work, and the inability to heal is mentally and physically stifling. I journaled a lot about healing. Every good day seemed to be followed by a bad day: blood draws, testing, appointments, exhaustion, and lots and lots of puking.

I reflect upon our healing since Ross's death. Healing is hard work. We go through rituals and routines, consciously and unconsciously. We celebrate small milestones and appreciate life differently. Reverence for life has taken on deeper meaning. I have become ever more aware of the passage of time.

For a while, we had a slogan when Ross was in the hospital. *Every day is one day closer to being home*. This slogan took on new meaning after Ross died. Many words had different interpretations after his death, fresh definitions arising like manna from holy ground, the bread of heaven.

After Ross died and all final measures of care were accounted for, I drove home alone. Ross had travelled between worlds, reaching a destination. I was making a journey between two worlds, merely forty-five miles apart. My car speakers sang to me, words of Leonard Cohen. *Eyes soft with sorrow, carrying a broken spirit…when she came back, she was nobody's wife*. Words that used to just be lyrics were now my reality. I was entering a world of grief work and life under reconstruction. I was wondering, simultaneously, who I was and who I would become.

Ross's primary physician said, "Don't let anyone tell you how to grieve." He recognized that each person with us on Ross's journey would be at a different place in his or her grief. Once again, there was the concept of permission to recognize grief and to work through it at an individual pace. These words were infinitely valuable and so true.

There were times when the nonreality that Ross had lived in was frustrating for me, especially as we lived in a reality that was a stark contrast to his. I now understand this nonreality as a gift, perhaps a coping or a hoping mechanism for him. As with the potato dent in the refrigerator, we can now think back to those times of his fantasizing and remember only the sweetness. The unpleasantness has disappeared.

There is a reality we face each day. There is a hole at the kitchen table, in his recliner, on the couch, the bed, the church pew, and the bleachers. His vehicle is gone. There is less laundry. In a sense, the hole formed slowly over time. In some ways, we had time to prepare and get used to what was to be. But there is also a hole in what is to be. There is a hole in the dreams we thought we knew. But we are still dreamers.

The concept of balance is exhausting. Life balance is talked about, written about, studied, and thought about a lot. It's something people strive for. I think about the rhythm of life, taking life and dealing with it as it's being lived, breathing in and out. I wonder if some of the most meaningful times in life aren't found when we're out of balance, when we are consumed, whether in ordinary or extraordinary experiences.

The Bible's book of Ecclesiastes tells us there is a time for every purpose under heaven when we focus on the task at hand. Time for work, rest, and play. Time for life and death. Time to breathe out and time to breathe in. Time to be out of balance in one direction and time to be in balance in another. There is a time when even our messes can become beautiful. We can turn our experience to treasure and know God's grace has been present in all of it.

Life is a miracle. Ross's life was framed with two extraordinary cancer experiences. He lived with fullness and gratitude in the time he was given. In life-changing ways, his endurance had an impact on all who surrounded him, and he made a difference.

September 11, 2010

Ross died last night. Absolute peace followed much suffering. As we look into the future, that was the moment that changed many lives. A couple weeks ago, I told Ross that he changed the world. He said, "No," and then smiled and said, "Well, maybe my part of it."

Thank you for being a part of Ross's world. The best way to remember Ross is to live and appreciate all that gives abundant life.

There is power in the passage of time. The door that went nowhere now goes somewhere. My lost keys were found. I have the recipe for Bunnie cake. There have been many more litters of pigs. Communion takes place the first Sunday of every month. Five All Saints' Sundays have passed since Ross's death. The garden outside UIHC has changed. The palliative care unit at UIHC has moved. Randy's still wearing a Ross wristband, and there is a band on my refrigerator that went through an Ironman race. The kids have moved forward in their lives. Chassis sleeps with me every night. I've conquered some real edges. I'm still me.

Shit still happens.

Everything is okay. In fact, there are many times I say, "All is well." I catch myself thinking about the normal things we do now, remembering times when life was so different.

There are times when we're guilty of taking our physical existence for granted. That is, until we witness or live an experience that causes us to put back into perspective the gift of physical life. We've witnessed the line between physical life and death. Death is as individual and unique as each person. We know that the combination of medicine, wisdom, and prayer can produce what we call miracles. Illness and hardship reawaken us to the gift and miracle of life, and we call ourselves blessed when we overcome obstacles.

Life is amazing, and we have constant reminders of both the frailty and strength of our physical existence on earth. This goes back as far as creation, which God deemed good. We are never more human than we are in the presence of death. We are never more Christian than when we recall God's triumph over death by the raising of his son, Jesus Christ.

Ross's grave is on the hill at St. John's Cemetery, close to the graves of his grandparents, close to where his parents will be buried. Inscribed on the back of Ross's tombstone are the words *Forever and Ever. Amen.* These words end the Lord's Prayer; they are in the Randy Travis song that was sung at Ross's funeral; and they remind us of the gift of eternal love.

• • •

It is with reverence that I share this story and what I believe.

I was born into the life of the church. For this I give thanks, first and foremost to my parents. Church has always been a part of me. My faith has grown, stagnated, and ebbed and flowed, often when least expected. Never has it disappeared, and never have I questioned the presence of God. Never.

These things ground my faith: Jesus cared for and about people. Jesus's life, death, and resurrection are the heart of the faith I claim.

I know about taking care of people. There are a lot of people I care for, worry about, and love. Caring is hard work. Sometimes it's intentional, and sometimes it just happens. It fills me with awe when I know I'm caring as Jesus would care. I love how our faith hovers around our actions, even when there are no words.

I have faith in the story of Jesus being the son of God. I know the questions. I don't have the answers, but I believe. That's all I need. There's room in me to handle the mystery.

I know there is a presence larger than human life, surrounding us, loving us, holding us. The grace of God is for each and every person.

God, hold us in the palm of your hand.
Empower us to do your work in the world.
Amen.

The Box

A MIME USES gestures to outline a box in the shape of a cube. Once the box is established, the mime struggles with it a bit but picks it up and moves it aside. Then the act continues.

All the documentation and medical paraphernalia I saved over the years of Ross's illnesses, surgeries, and hospitalizations would fit neatly into a box. This stuff tells a story about a portion of time. This stuff spurs vivid memories and emotions. The box holds treasures, both of blessing and burden. But the real content is not about stuff.

Imagine me holding the box. I'm picking it up and moving it aside. It is no longer center stage, but the lid will always be open.

I am indebted to the doctor who gave me the box image. I find it even more meaningful as years have passed. The doctor told me there would be a time when I would feel as if the experiences of those years had been placed in a box and moved aside. He mimed this as he told me, stating that this boxing up would evolve without my consciously realizing it. And it did. Disturbing memories have subsided as sweetness has replaced them. None of it is forgotten; it is just set aside in a box with an open lid.

At first, content escaped at unexpected, unpredictable times. It now seems less overwhelming when memories creep out of that box. Life is different now.

The box and its contents will always be a part of me. Forever and ever.

Bibliography

Duck, Ruth C. *Bread for the Journey.* New York: The Pilgrim Press, 1981.

Harwick, Henry J. *Forty-Four Years with the Mayo Clinic: 1908–1952.* Rochester, MN: Mayo Foundation for Medical Education and Research, 2012.

Havel, Vaclav. *Disturbing the Peace.* New York: Alfred A. Knopf, 1990.

Norris, Kathleen. *The Quotidian Mysteries, Laundry, Liturgy and "Women's Work."* Mahwah, NJ: Paulist Press, 1998.

Nouwen, Henri J. M. *Mornings with Henri J. M. Nouwen.* Ann Arbor, MI: Servant Publications, 1997.

"Popular Quotes." Goodreads. Accessed May 9, 2015. http://www.goodreads.com/quotes/.

Seuss, Dr. *Oh, the Places You'll Go!* New York: Random House, 1988.

Made in the USA
San Bernardino, CA
22 June 2017